Convincing, plenty of how-to, apt analogies, and
community, Drexler's guidance to Christian sch
hands, not on their shelves.
—Dan Vander Ark, former Executive Director
Christian Schools International

Teachers are the heart of the Christian school learning community, and Jim
Drexler's wonderful new book lays out a plan, supported by current research,
for nurturing both novice and veteran teachers. Building on the foundation
of *Schools as Communities* [Colorado Springs, CO: Purposeful Design Publications, 2007], Drexler lays out a comprehensive plan for fostering growth
within the context of a professional learning community.

This book will be an excellent text for educational leadership programs and for
heads of schools who are looking for an effective way to work with their teachers.
—Bruce Hekman, Professor of Education
Calvin College

This book serves as an excellent counterpart to the 2007 Drexler-edited book,
Schools as Communities [Colorado Springs, CO: Purposeful Design Publications, 2007]. Here Drexler focuses on the key issue of how to build and nourish Christian community, particularly as regards the new teacher.

Research shows that, in both American and Canadian schools (including
Christian schools), the attrition rate among new teachers is at least 30 percent
in the first three years. Why this is and how schools can counter this sad waste
of human teaching potential is the central focus of Drexler's book.

Drexler tackles this issue in a holistic manner, situating it in the need for
schools to become professional learning communities. The writing is clear and
focused, and this book is a fine example of the dictum that *Christian educational principles must be practical while Christian educational practice must be
principled*. I highly recommend this book for school-based leaders and school
board members, and as a text in Christian educational leadership courses and
programs at colleges and universities.
—Robert W. Bruinsma, Professor of Education Emeritus
The King's University College

A successful, transformative Christian school community exemplifies the biblical mandate to "love your neighbor as yourself" in the various relationships that are intrinsic to the Christian school experience. Jim Drexler makes a strong and compelling case in *Nurturing the School Community* for intentional, sustainable, and collaborative faculty communities that enable teachers to learn, grow, and take personal responsibility for advancing high-quality teaching and professional growth. This comprehensive and practical approach to building faculty communities through new-teacher induction and professional learning communities will serve as an invaluable road map for Christian school leaders who are serious about effectively nurturing new teachers and building community within their faculty culture.

—James Marsh, Head of School
Westminster Christian Academy, St. Louis, Missouri

Every Christian school is blessed with teaching excellence. Unfortunately, that excellence is too-often random and disconnected from other classrooms in the school. The development of professional learning communities is a critical step toward connecting excellence from classroom to classroom—a must for the twenty-first-century Christian school.

—Dave Koetje, President and CEO
Christian Schools International

Of all professional educators, Christians should be the most committed to strong and effective induction and development of teachers and administrators in their schools. This is not always the case. Thankfully, Jim Drexler not only provides the rationale for why we should support the development of our teachers but provides ample instruction as to how to go about this important activity. *Nurturing the School Community* will be a significant resource for those concerned about strengthening the capacities of educators to teach, serve, and lead well.

—Scot Headley, Chair
Department of Educational Foundations and Leadership, George Fox University

Nurturing the School Community

Nurturing the School Community

Teacher Induction and Professional Learning Communities

James L. Drexler

purposeful design®
p u b l i c a t i o n s

Colorado Springs, Colorado

Purposeful Design Publications is the publishing division of the Association of Christian Schools International (ACSI) and is committed to the ministry of Christian school education, to enable Christian educators and schools worldwide to effectively prepare students for life. As the publisher of textbooks, trade books, and other educational resources within ACSI, Purposeful Design Publica-tions strives to produce biblically sound materials that reflect Christian scholarship and stewardship and that address the identified needs of Christian schools around the world.

The views expressed in this publication are those of the author, and they may not necessarily represent the position of the Association of Christian Schools International. References to books, websites, and other ancillary resources are not endorsements by ACSI. These materials were selected by the author to provide readers with additional resources appropriate to the concepts addressed in this book.

All Scripture quotations are taken from the Holy Bible, NEW INTERNATIONAL VERSION®. Copyright © 1973, 1978, 1984 by Biblica, Inc. All rights reserved worldwide. Used by permission.

Printed in the United States of America
20 19 18 17 16 15 14 13 12 11   1 2 3 4 5 6 7

Library of Congress Cataloging-in-Publication Data

Drexler, James L.
   Nurturing the school community : teacher induction and professional learning communities / James L. Drexler.
      p. cm.
   Includes bibliographical references.
   ISBN 978-1-58331-383-1 (pbk.)
  1. Teacher orientation. 2. Mentoring in education. 3. Professional learning communities.
I. Title.
   LB1729.D74 2011
   371.102--dc23
                                        2011020469

Catalog #6624

Design team: Bethany Kerstetter, Mike Riester
Editorial team: Cheryl Chiapperino, Gina Brandon, John Conaway

Purposeful Design Publications
A Division of ACSI
PO Box 65130 • Colorado Springs CO 80962-5130
Customer Service: 800-367-0798 • www.acsi.org

For Max Peter Schimpf—our first grandchild, who was named in honor of his maternal grandfather, Max Belz, a hero for Christian schooling.

Contents

Acknowledgments

As this book and the earlier book *Schools as Communities* both argue, none of us operates in a vacuum. So as the author, I am happy to thank the many people who have encouraged and supported this work.

Specifically, Steve Babbitt, the executive director for Purposeful Design Publications, has consistently encouraged and supported my work over the past six years, offering insightful help and caution along the way. More important, he has become a trusted friend, and I hope one day to hit a golf ball as well as he does.

I also want to thank Cheryl Chiapperino for her excellent and meticulous work as editor for this book. Her thorough and thoughtful work has made this a far better book than it would have been otherwise.

To all those master of education students whom I have had the privilege of teaching over these years at Covenant College, I thank you for your scholarly work and for the many valuable things you have taught me as we have discussed induction, professional learning communities, and many other topics during our wonderful summers on Lookout Mountain.

Finally, to my bride of thirty-one years, I want to thank Sara not only for her proofreading of this book's draft but for her love and support for work like this. She is a product of Christian schooling and a trophy of God's amazing grace, and my children are loved by Jesus. What else could a man want!

To God be the glory.

Introduction

Sam was a natural in the classroom. Having a deep belly laugh, a captivating baritone voice, a strong intellect, and a love for children, he was a great addition to our school. He was well trained, having earned both a bachelor's degree and a master's degree in his field. And since he had played college basketball, he was a logical choice for a coaching position. As the only teacher who brought diversity to our otherwise all-white faculty, this friendly and eager six-foot-four African American man was a school administrator's dream hire.

And teaching and coaching are exactly what we assigned to him: daily, six sections (out of seven periods) of teaching that required four preparations and eventually, nearly one hundred fifty students, many of whom were freshmen—since he was so personable and popular. Added to this load was coaching the JV boys' and girls' basketball teams and serving on several committees (after all, we thought, "Don't we want to expose the new black teacher to as many of our students and parents as possible?"). And Sam was a willing and hard worker, never one to say no or "That's too much." He worked long hours during the week and sometimes even longer over the weekends in a vain attempt to keep up with all the grading and other paperwork.

By the way, Sam received no induction and no formal mentoring other than the on-again, off-again contact with his department head. After one year of teaching, Sam left, and to this day, over twenty-five years later, he has not returned to the classroom. Sam was a classic case of burnout, or as some call it "new-teacher hazing": practices and policies that result in new teachers experiencing poorer working conditions than what their veteran colleagues experience.

Some might hear this account and conclude that this unfortunate incident happened twenty years ago—that things have certainly improved since then. In some schools perhaps they have, but the statistics indicate that, by and large, effective and comprehensive induction and mentoring programs are still few and far between, particularly in Christian schools. On top of not being effectively inducted and mentored, new teachers are often overloaded with too many preps, given some of the more difficult classes and students, and assigned extra duties that frequently exacerbate the already-existing feelings of inadequacy, fear, uncertainty, and frustration. It's no wonder that many first- and second-year teachers quit the profession. Educational leaders, therefore, find themselves coconspirators in perpetuating an unjust and inhumane practice: programming new teachers for failure. It's not surprising that "some observers have dubbed education 'the profession that eats its young'" (Halford 1998, 33).

"In the 1999–2000 school year, approximately 500,000 public and private school teachers left the teaching profession, with more than 123,000 of them attributing their departure to a lack of appropriate administrative support (Ingersoll 2002). Nearly one-fourth of new teachers leave the profession after only two years, and one-third leave after three years (Ingersoll 2002)" (Millinger 2004). A research report cosponsored by the Center for the Study of Teaching and Policy and the Consortium for Policy Research in Education paints an even bleaker picture by asserting that almost 50 percent of new teachers leave the profession within five years, a staggering statistic that has titanic financial and academic implications for schools (Ingersoll 2003).

Some argue that not enough new teachers are entering the market, suggesting that the teacher shortages are due to sheer numbers. Recent national studies, however, including the Schools and Staffing Survey and the Teacher Follow-up Survey (both administered by the National Center for Education Statistics), indicate that the annual scramble for teachers is negatively affected by the high attrition among new teachers. New teachers who leave the profession identify (1) job dissatisfaction and (2) the pursuit of other careers as key factors in their decision to quit teaching. Trying just to recruit new teachers without addressing new-teacher attrition is, as Richard Ingersoll and Thomas Smith note, like pouring more water into a bucket filled with holes (2003, 33).

Christian schools ought to be the vanguard of building strong relationships and community. One essential way of pursuing this is to ensure that our new teachers are supported and nurtured so that each one can become an effective educator. This building of community by supporting and nourishing teachers is what this book is all about. And obviously, novice teachers need opportunities to grow professionally, improve their skills, learn from mistakes, and work in trusting and supportive contexts alongside colleagues in order to grow as teachers. Regrettably, most new teachers are simply given their books and curriculum; shown to their classroom; loaded down with numerous preps, students, and responsibilities; and given only token forms of support at best. It's not surprising, then, when we learn that new teachers quit the profession at an alarming rate. At the same time, veteran teachers need to grow and improve, and together with novice teachers, need to be formed into vibrant professional learning communities, which will lead to stronger schools and higher levels of learning for our students.

We can do much better in Christian schools. We must.

First Things First: Cultivating Community

Now about brotherly love we do not need to write to you, for you yourselves have been taught by God to love each other. And in fact, you do love all the brothers throughout Macedonia. Yet we urge you, brothers, *to do so more and more.*   —1 Thessalonians 4:9–10, emphasis added

Community is at the heart of our faith. The Bible declares that we are created for community, we are redeemed for community, and we will live eternally in community.

Biblical Framework

Richard Mouw writes of a New Jersey man traveling in the South for the first time. After considering the menu options for breakfast, and noting that several combination meals featured grits, he asked the waitress, "'Miss, what is a grit?' She replied, 'Honey, they don't come by *themselves!*'" Mouw concludes, "Like grits, 'Christian' is a plural thing. To follow Jesus is to be part of a community" (2004, 65–66).

The apostle Peter makes a remarkable and descriptive claim when he states that Christians are "a chosen people, a royal priesthood, a holy nation ... the people of God" (1 Peter 2:9–10). It is instructive that Peter does not refer to a chosen person, a single priest, or an individual citizen. When people are saved by grace, Jesus calls them into a spiritual family, a church, a kingdom. As Stanley Grenz writes, "Community—or more fully stated, persons-in-relationship—is the central, organizing concept of theological construction, the theme around which a systematic theology is structured" (2000, 214–15).

Some of God's first recorded words in Scripture—as readers eavesdrop on a heavenly conversation—express a relationship: "Let *us* make man in *our* image, in *our* likeness" (Genesis 1:26, emphasis added). The triune God—Father, Son, and Holy Spirit—exists eternally in community; and humans, created in God's image, reflect that relational, social quality.

As the story of salvation unfolds, God deals first with the families of Abraham, Isaac, and Jacob. He later creates the nation of Israel. Eventually the church is established, the community of God's people (Ephesians 2:11–22). John envisions the culmination of this theme as a new heaven and a new earth in which a redeemed body of believers live together for all eternity, reconciled with God, with one another, and with creation. In a very real sense, then, one cannot fully understand redemption, the church, and the kingdom of God without understanding, appreciating, and living in community. (Drexler 2007, xiv–xv)

And schools are communities, "collections of individuals who are bonded together by natural will and who are together bound to a set of shared ideas and ideals" (Sergiovanni 1996, 48). Therefore as this book discusses new teachers, comprehensive induction, and professional learning communities, it is centered in a fundamental biblical concept that Christians ought to live and work together. "As a Christian teacher, therefore, you consciously strive to forge your classroom into a learning *community* in which students experience the richness of living in a caring and supportive but also challenging environment" (Van Brummelen 2009, 179). And this same model should be pursued for the school as a whole, as students and educators learn together.

The Bible declares that humans are made in God's image and likeness, so it follows that people are created to live and work in community. Christians are part of a family, members of the Church, citizens in a nation, employees and employers, and students and teachers. Everywhere one looks, there is community, fellowship, relationships—at least the structures for it—and it is within these community relationships that God's design and purpose for human beings is manifested.

To be sure, American individualism and humankind's sinful condition constantly work against these ideals, but the Bible is clear that Christians need each other in community and fellowship to grow, flourish, and find fulfillment. It is within relationships that people reflect the social image of God.

Dietrich Bonhoeffer

Dietrich Bonhoeffer, the German Lutheran pastor who was executed in a Nazi concentration camp in 1945 just days before liberation, writes about what it means to live together in community. In *Life Together*, Bonhoeffer observes this about the fallen nature of humankind: "But the important thing is that a Christian community should know that somewhere in it there will certainly be 'a reasoning among them, which of them should be the greatest.' It is the struggle of the natural man for self-justification. He finds it only in comparing himself with others, in condemning and judging others. Self-justification and judging go together, as justification by grace and serving others go together" (1954, 91). In other words if we truly understand, believe, and accept justification by grace through faith, then serving others in humility and love is the logical consequence.

"Christianity means community through Jesus Christ and in Jesus Christ" (Bonhoeffer 1954, 21). What Bonhoeffer means is that Christians need one another (Romans 12:5–8, 1 Corinthians 12:12–30), that Christians are able to come to one another only through Jesus, and that this mystical bond has been created for all of eternity. This union between Christians is not an ideal for the future but a present spiritual reality. Bonhoeffer says, "Because Christ has long since acted decisively for my brother, before I could begin to act, I must leave him his freedom to be Christ's; I must meet him only as the person *that he already is in Christ's eyes*" (36, emphasis added). This has colossal implications for how Christian educators should regard and treat one another.

What changes for the good might occur if educators learned to see each other as God views them in Christ? What would happen if instead of looking at so-and-so and thinking, "He's the one who lied" or "She's the one who broke her promise" or "They're the ones who stole something" or "He's the one who causes the trouble"—in other words, labeling fellow Christians by their sins and failures—Christian educators began to look at one another and see what Jesus sees: a forgiven, loved, and blessed child of God who is *right now* clothed with Christ's righteousness? Without a doubt, criticism, pride, put-downs, mistrust, egos, and backbiting—all of these and more would be turned into helping, blessing, listening, giving, respecting, forgiving, loving, and being collegial.

In Romans 12:3, Paul commands us to look at ourselves with sober judgment. Paul's use of the Greek language in effect says that those who think of themselves more highly than they ought—who desire first place in the Kingdom and "build" themselves up by tearing others down—are actually displaying a form of insanity.[1] He argues that if Christians understand who they are as fallen sinners in need of God's mercy, they will learn to understand their dependence on Jesus and their need for one another. From verse 10 on, Paul continues his admonition by commanding Christians to be devoted to one another in brotherly love, and in so doing they will by definition begin to think of others above self. Believers are frequently described in Scripture as a family, an intimate and tender group of people bound to one another by the Lord Jesus Christ. Christian educators, therefore, by God's grace ought to demonstrate devotion and tender affection to one another. As Paul says elsewhere, "Be completely humble and gentle; be patient, bearing with one another in love" (Ephesians 4:2).

One practical way Bonhoeffer suggests showing love and humility is in controlling the tongue: "Thus it must be a decisive rule of every Christian fellowship that each individual is *prohibited from saying much that occurs to him*" (1954, 92; emphasis added). What a change there would be in our self-referenced, Facebook-dominated, Twitter-soaked, blog-infested culture in which people feel free to chatter and gossip around the clock. What a breath of fresh air it would be for Christian schools, especially in the faculty lounge, if educators learned by God's grace to be "quick to listen, slow to speak" (James

1:19). As this cultural change occurs in community, a Christian "will make a matchless discovery. He will be able to cease from constantly scrutinizing the other person, judging him, condemning him, putting him in his particular place where he can gain ascendancy over him and thus doing violence to him as a person" (Bonhoeffer 1954, 92–93).

Relationships

"Then God said, 'Let us make man in our image, in our likeness'" (Genesis 1:26). "The Lord God said, 'It is not good for the man to be alone'" (2:18). These two statements present the biblical command for people to live, work, and serve in relationship with one another. Simply put, human begins are created, designed, and mandated to thrive and grow in the context of community. Community is as much a part of the original creational order as the sun, moon, and stars; the cycle of seasons; marriage; or any of the other norms of creation.

In addition, human beings are created with four primary relationships: with God, with others, with self, and with nature. One can only imagine how beautifully this must have functioned in the Garden of Eden before sin entered the world, how Adam and Eve were able to live and flourish in seamless relationships with all four in perfect harmony. The Fall, however, radically altered and corrupted everything, including these fundamental relationships:

+ Since *God* is holy, righteous, and without sin, all human beings, as unrighteous lawbreakers, discover that their relationship with God is broken, and as Paul comprehensively argues in Romans 1:18–3:19, everyone is guilty and without excuse. As sinners, we construct our own idols to worship, pursue self-justification, and build our own leaky cisterns after forsaking God (Jeremiah 2:13).
+ People know intuitively that all relationships with *others* are fractured, because everywhere there are divisions, conflict, hatred, strife, injustice, racism, and fear.
+ As a result of the Fall, individuals can't get along with even *themselves* anymore, because all are subject to self-deception, shame, anxiety, low self-esteem, doubt, and restlessness.
+ Finally, the realities of the Fall result in pollution, materialism, and a variety of other exploitations of the *natural created order* that God commands us to be good stewards of in Genesis 1:28. Even the soil now produces weeds!

The beauty of redemption is that each of these corrupted and distorted relationships can be restored and renewed through Jesus Christ. Our personal salvation is an important and significant event, but the full redemptive story that pictures the ultimate restoration and reconciliation of all things (Colossians 1:15–20) gives us hope for Christian community. "And he died for all, that those who live should no longer live for themselves" (2 Corinthians 5:15). This understanding of the Creation-Fall-Redemption framework of the history of salvation brings into focus why relationships are so important for Christian educators.

How can things be different in our Christian schools? By God's grace, teachers can begin to keep their opinions to themselves, learn to defer to others, look for practical and tangible ways to demonstrate love and compassion for one another, and stop keeping a record of wrongs against one another. A change like this will have a tremendous impact on what and how teachers teach. It will also change approaches to classroom management and discipline. This does not imply, of course, that teachers stop teaching the truth or that students are discouraged from asking questions and engaging in discussion. Both grace and truth are indispensable for learning.

As these changes happen, students will see new attitudes modeled by teachers and administrators and will be encouraged to treat one another respectfully and lovingly on the basis of the respect and love they have received. Finally, building godly, grace-filled relationships and community will become one of the most important goals of the school. "The vision is, first, that the school will be a *community*, a place full of adults and students who care about, look after, and root for one another and who work together for the good of the whole, in times of need and in times of celebration" (Barth 2002, 11; emphasis added).

This is an exciting image of the kingdom of God: first the changed hearts of individuals, then the obvious effects of that conversion in the lives of others through relationships, and ultimately the transformation of systems and institutions by the grace of God. It's a revolutionary vision that is packaged in humility, patience, joy, mercy, sacrifice, and compassion, because relationships are messy, but God's grace is sufficient.

Note

1. The King James Version of Romans 12:3 tells us to "think soberly." The definition of the Greek word for *soberly* is "to *be of sound mind*, i.e., *sane*" (Strong n.d., 945 in "Main Concordance," 70 in "The Greek Dictionary of the New Testament").

Fostering Growth: The Needs of Novice and Veteran Teachers

The righteous will flourish like a palm tree, they will grow like a cedar of
Lebanon.   —Psalm 92:12

Before considering the specifics of comprehensive induction and professional
learning communities (PLCs), it's helpful to first consider what a school is
looking for in an effective teacher. Most everyone has experienced a memorable
educator, that excellent teacher who made a life-changing impact, or who at
least caused students to remember him or her as "the best teacher." What are
the attributes of these effective, high-quality, excellent teachers? As teaching
vacancies occur, for whom should principals look?

Effective Teachers

Many studies of effective teachers tend to look at easy-to-measure criteria—
categories like teacher certification, academic degrees, and experience. Some
studies (Gitomer 2007; Rice 2003; Ferguson 1998; Strauss and Sawyer 1986)
establish a link between teachers' test scores and test scores of the teachers'
students, assuming that the teachers who scored higher on standardized tests

are more apt to help their students achieve. In some content areas like math and science, research has also shown that high levels of content knowledge about the subject taught can translate to a positive impact on student learning. A 2001 research report prepared for the U.S. Department of Education (Wilson, Floden, and Ferrini-Mundy) concluded that subject-matter preparation, pedagogical instruction in a teacher preparation program, and practice teaching all contribute positively to the development of quality teachers. In a blistering response to a U.S. secretary's annual report on teacher quality— in which the secretary dismisses most teacher preparation programs and certification requirements as "burdensome" and "broken"—Linda Darling-Hammond and Peter Youngs cite dozens of research projects that demonstrate something quite different:

> Looking across studies, several aspects of teachers' qualifications have been found to bear some relationship to student achievement. These include teachers' (a) general academic and verbal ability; (b) subject matter knowledge; (c) knowledge about teaching and learning as reflected in teacher education courses or preparation experiences; (d) teaching experience; and (e) the combined set of qualifications measured by teacher certification, which includes most of the preceding factors (Darling-Hammond 2000). (2002, 16)

Not surprisingly, Patrick Bassett, president of the National Association of Independent Schools—an organization of private schools, some of which pride themselves on *not* hiring certified teachers—cites research by the Abell Foundation claiming that certification and teacher preparation programs do not guarantee quality teaching: "It's easier to help new teachers learn *how* to teach well— using strong mentoring systems—than to teach them *what* to teach" (2003). Bassett also notes the argument that qualities such as knowledge, passion, and love for students have more to do with student achievement. Since there are arguments on both sides, though, it seems wise to avoid both extremes—either a rigid bureaucracy of teacher education requirements or a complete abandonment of all teaching requirements—as schools look for the best teachers.

Part of the difficulty is that teaching is a complex activity and in some ways is more an art than a science. Malcolm Gladwell, author of best-selling books like *Blink, Tipping Point,* and *Outliers,* wrote a provocative article for the *New Yorker* in which he compared the NFL's drafting of college quarterbacks to the hiring of new teachers, concluding that neither is an exact science. Gladwell carelessly concludes that "teaching should be open to anyone with a pulse and a college degree" and argues that new hires should be included in a lengthy "apprenticeship system" before being fully hired (2008). Writing for a Christian Schools International blog, Barry Koops (2009) offers a more balanced perspective based on Gladwell's insights, encouraging principals to do the following:

+ "Cast the net more widely when considering beginning teachers."
+ "Recruit aggressively and widely [when] considering that finding, hiring, developing great teachers is their most important task."
+ Make "frequent and thorough" teacher observations.
+ Require "evidence of 'value added'" to annual evaluations.
+ Establish the first two years of teaching as provisional.
+ Require from all teachers a "written professional improvement plan that includes performance goals and professional growth activities."
+ Provide evidence of teacher performance for accreditation.

Finally, Teach for America, a nonprofit organization that recruits college graduates to teach for two years in low-income schools, has been the subject of ongoing internal and external research to determine why some of these non-certified teachers are so successful. Among the characteristics of these effective teachers are the following (Ripley 2010):

+ High expectations for all students
+ Constant assessment of their students and themselves
+ An undistracted focus on student achievement
+ Solid planning and preparation based on teaching goals
+ Clear routines that are so strong they run without the teacher present
+ Perseverance in college (the last couple of years' credit hours most significant) and in life—"grit" (Often, excellent teachers succeed after early failures.)
+ Successful leaders in college and in life
+ Life satisfaction—contentment
+ Deep subject knowledge

Having all of these characteristics in mind, Christian school administrators should begin by first conducting their own research among the faculty in their school, seeking to determine the characteristics manifested by the high-quality educators already teaching. Chances are, some of the same attributes described above will show up among this group of excellent teachers. Creating a set of attributes necessary for excellence on the basis of the culture and climate of an individual school and community could go a long way in helping identify which teacher candidates should be hired for that school. Indispensable to this process as administrators consider new hires are thorough interviews, background checks, trial-teaching experience, and perhaps some form of personality-profile testing.

Novice Teachers and Adult Learners

A central argument of this book is that the work to make seamless transitions from pre-service clinical practice (during college) to the first few years of novice teaching (with comprehensive induction) to career-long quality teaching and growth (through PLCs) is a crucially important leadership process that takes intentional time and effort.

Despite the strength of their teacher preparation programs, teachers new to the profession come to the classroom with many fears, uncertainties, doubts, and questions. Even though new teachers are professionals who may have earned certification, they need opportunities to grow professionally and develop into effective teachers. Teachers (like professionals in other fields), according to Charlotte Danielson and Thomas McGreal (2000), "need time to improve their skills under the watchful eye of experts—and time to reflect, learn from mistakes, and work with colleagues as they acquire good judgment and tacit knowledge about teaching and learning" (Black 2004). New teachers in particular have strong emotional needs along with desires for security, acceptance, and assurance (Doerger 2003). They also need help in developing effective lesson and unit plans, plans for sequential learning, a variety of classroom-management techniques, and other skills in the art of teaching.

The Santa Cruz New Teacher Project, led by the University of California–Santa Cruz since 1988, has determined that "new teachers move though several phases: from anticipation, to survival, to disillusionment, to rejuvenation, to reflection, then back to anticipation" (Moir 2000, 18). One of the important roles of school leaders, therefore, is to "assist new teachers and ease the transition from student teacher to full-time professional" (22). Further, "recent research shows that most beginning teachers learn through an 'idiosyncratic process' that is actually more in keeping with constructivist theories of learning—and more like the surgeon's learning curve" (Black 2004). Another analogy is that the first years of teaching can be viewed as a period of grieving—"one must give up utopian dreams of teaching for a time to adjust ideals with reality" (Johnson 2004).

"The major concerns of most new teachers include classroom management, student motivation, differentiation for individual student needs, assessment and evaluation of learning, and dealing effectively with parents" (Renard 2003, 63). Another key need of new teachers (and experienced teachers as well) is intellectual stimulation since effective and successful practitioners are lifelong learners. New teachers must learn to view teaching as a creative art, understand how and when to take risks, experience the satisfaction of personal relationships within community, and realize the importance of professional growth. "The ongoing challenges, the creativity inherent in the teaching process, and the round-the-clock learning are significant forces in the rejuvenation of our best teachers" (Williams 2003, 72).

In 2003, one hundred forty teachers in six districts were interviewed through the Georgia Systemic Teacher Education Program and were asked what most helps beginning teachers. Their responses follow in rank order:

1. Giving new teachers the opportunity to observe other teachers.
2. Assigning mentors to new teachers.
3. Providing new teachers with feedback based on classroom observations.
4. Providing new teachers with co-planning time with other teachers.
5. Assigning new teachers to smaller classes. (Gilbert 2005)

One of the distinctive characteristics of effective teachers is the skill of what Jacob Kounin calls "withitness" (1970, 74), the awareness an experienced teacher has of all that is happening in the classroom. Others have labeled this phenomenon as "having eyes in the back of her head." A clever scene in the 2008 movie *Doubt* (written and directed by John Patrick Shanley) captures this idea. Sister Aloysius, the principal of a Catholic school in New York in the 1960s, advises Sister James, a new teacher in the school, to hang a picture of the pope at the top of the chalkboard. When Sister James protests that the framed picture isn't of the current pope, Sister Aloysius says that it doesn't matter which pope it is since the purpose of the picture is to allow Sister James to see her students while she is writing on the chalkboard. Later, a frequently naughty student sneaks out of his seat while Sister James is writing on the board, and he is stunned when she catches him in the act (by seeing his reflection in the pope's picture).

Withitness, although usually associated with effective classroom management and prevention of discipline problems, has come to be more inclusively used to describe how student behavior and student work function together to give the teacher important cues. As a form of "reflection-in-action," a teacher perceives cues from students, ponders what those cues mean, and then makes decisions and modifications while at the same time continuing with instruction (Schön 1987). This task is difficult to master, and most beginning teachers do not accomplish it easily. Withitness is an acquired skill that takes practice, dedication, reflection, and the assistance of others.

Related to the development of withitness is the concept of "flow" described by Mihaly Csikszentmihalyi: "the sense of effortless action" that people "feel in moments that stand out as the best in their lives" (1997, 29). For "flow" to occur for teachers, they need "clear goals, skills to meet the level of challenge, and immediate feedback" (Williams 2003, 72), all features that can be facilitated through mentoring and induction.

Coupled with all of this is the reality that beginning teachers are adults, so effective mentoring, induction, and professional development plans need to be done in light of *andragogy*, "the philosophy of adult education." According to Malcolm Knowles (1980), the father of andragogy, adults learn in different ways than children do, so at least four main principles need to be considered:
1. Adults need to know why they are learning or doing something and how it will directly affect them.
2. Adults bring their own lifetime experiences that should be tapped as a resource for their continued learning along with a recognition that "one size" *doesn't* fit all.

3. Adults tend to be hands-on learners (problem solving as opposed to rote memorization).
4. Adults want and need to apply new knowledge immediately.

Educational leaders must be aware of these differences, look for opportunities to activate adult learning, and explore ways to facilitate this learning. They must know that facilitating adult learning requires

> acknowledging and valuing what teachers bring with them from their cultural and historical communities.... For teachers, then, learning does not occur in some unrelated workshop unconnected to the particular learning situation in which the teacher works. Building a professional community means taking seriously [the idea] that learning for teachers occurs in the school, in the context of learning, and focusing on the particular learning needs and contributions of teachers. (Matthews and Crow 2010, 64)

In summary, new teachers bring a variety of needs and expectations into the school, so the need for effective comprehensive induction programs and for the development of PLCs is critical. "To stay in teaching, today's—and tomorrow's—teachers need school conditions where they are successful and supported, opportunities to work with other educators in professional learning communities rather than in isolation, differentiated leadership and advancement prospects during the course of the career, and good pay for what they do" (Cochran-Smith 2004, 391).

New-Teacher Attrition—and Why It's a Problem

A traumatic event for any school community occurs when a new teacher quits or decides not to return, a decision that harms the culture of the school, impedes the learning of students, and negatively affects the budget. According to research, one in every three new teachers will quit the profession before his or her third year of teaching, and in some locations the average is closer to one in two. Every situation is unique, but the reasons new teachers quit fall into six predictable categories:

1. Each school has its own unique *culture* (values, priorities, "how we do it here") and *climate* (atmosphere, personality, "how it feels here"). Despite the best efforts of administrators and prospective faculty, sometimes there simply isn't a good match and the new teacher doesn't fit.

2. Many teachers who choose not to return to a school speak of a *lack of administrative support*. This issue will be addressed in more detail in chapters 3 and 4, but multiple levels of support, encouragement, professional development opportunities, evaluation, and counsel can go a long way in helping new teachers grow, mature, flourish—and want to stay where they are.

3. The most commonly mentioned dissatisfaction among first-year teachers is their *struggles with classroom management*. Unfortunately, school administrators are either too busy or simply unaware of this widespread frustration, and consequently they allow teachers to "learn from their mistakes" when instead the administrators could take proactive steps to (a) require new teachers to observe model classrooms, (b) invite new teachers to regular meetings in which they are free to express their struggles while receiving practical advice from veterans, and (c) use video instruction on effective classroom procedures.

4. One inexplicable oddity of many schools is that new teachers are frequently given the *worst teaching assignments*, the least desirable classrooms, the broken and used equipment—the "new teacher hazing" mentioned in the introduction. "Placing new teachers in the most challenging classrooms without comprehensive induction ... is like putting new licensed drivers in the top heat of a NASCAR race" (Alliance for Excellent Education 2004, 2).

5. Many new teachers "don't know what they don't know" as they start their career. The multiple demands from students, parents, colleagues, administrators, and others can be daunting along with daily lesson planning, grading, meetings, difficult classes, and a host of other *disillusions*. Together these demands and disillusions can culminate in leading a new teacher to quit the profession. No administrator can eliminate either the workload or the expectations for teachers, but he or she can take steps to enable new teachers to navigate from this level of disappointment and disillusionment to the level of becoming effective teachers.

6. Regrettably, most schools are designed in ways that encourage *isolation, loneliness*, and *competition*. These issues will be discussed further in chapters 5 and 6, but the most effective antidote to these symptoms is the development of vibrant PLCs that fold in novice teachers with veterans.

Why does new-teacher attrition matter? There are numerous negative implications:

1. Constant turnover makes community building problematic and leads to inconsistency, loss of momentum, and negative morale among the faculty.

2. The impetus for ongoing school improvement is curtailed by a revolving door among the teaching staff.

3. Teacher attrition costs money. Harry Wong estimates that each teacher who leaves during the first three years can cost over $50,000 once all the time and expenses of replacing that teacher are accounted for (2003, 20).

4. Most important, student learning suffers negatively as students are exposed repeatedly to inexperienced and unseasoned teachers, and as needed improvements in the curriculum and in pedagogy are stalled.

Working with a Multigenerational Faculty

Although schools are unique in many ways, it is likely that almost every Christian school has a teaching faculty that crosses generational lines. Some veteran teachers come from the Baby Boomer Generation, while younger teachers and novice teachers probably come from Generations X and Y. Although it can be dangerous to overgeneralize and pigeonhole teachers into certain categories, the chart on the next two pages demonstrates some of the commonly held distinctions between these three generations along with some implications for educational leaders as they seek to recruit and retain Generation Y teachers.

Table 1. Generational distinctions and implications

Baby Boomer Generation (1943–1960)— also known as baby boomers	Generation X (1961–1981)— also known as Gen Xers	Generation Y (1981–2003)— also known as Gen Yers, or millennials	Implications for administrators of Generation Y teachers
Made the paradigm shift into technology	Created technology	Grew up digitally	New teachers are tech savvy but maybe not as strong in written-, verbal-, and nonverbal-communication skills.
Are respectful of authority	Have a growing distrust of authority figures	Desire to trust authority	New teachers demand transparency in management.
Provide cordial and directive leadership	Challenge authority; ask why	Desire competent leaders they can admire and trust	New teachers want authentic and distributed leadership in schools.
View work as an obligation	View work as a difficult challenge	Desire meaningful employment; view work as a means to an end	New teachers want to have significant leadership responsibilities.
Have had a career in one or two places	Willing to change jobs frequently	Want to "get ahead" quickly	New teachers want encouragement toward advanced degrees and promotions.
Work alone more often	Value individualism and pragmatism	Desire to work with other bright and creative people	New teachers are more apt to thrive in professional learning communities and small mentoring groups.
Don't want feedback; prefer title and money	Don't look over their shoulders; fun is serious business	Desire constant feedback and recognition as equals	New teachers want quick responses to e-mails.

Baby Boomer Generation (1943–1960)— also known as baby boomers	Generation X (1961–1981)— also known as Gen Xers	Generation Y (1981–2003)— also known as Gen Yers, or millennials	Implications for administrators of Generation Y teachers
Dislike change	Accept change	Look for ways to precipitate change, which they expect and find exciting	New teachers need opportunities to introduce new programs and methods.
Are accustomed to a male-dominated workplace	Are accustomed to the Sexual Revolution	Are accustomed to a workplace more dominated by females	Administrators need to be cautious about stereotyping or making assumptions.
Need to feel valued and wanted	Value individual freedom; "Do it your way!"	Need to be convinced; desire an enjoyable work environment	Administrators should understand that recruiting becomes more of a "sales job" about the school.
Demonstrate optimism	Demonstrate skepticism	Demonstrate realism	Administrators should demonstrate honesty and openness in communication.
Buy now, pay later	Are more conservative	Earn to spend	Administrators should understand that working conditions are more important; they need to keep employees satisfied.
Are workaholics; career focused	Get the work done	Wonder what's next; love a challenge; are entrepreneurial	Administrators should create opportunities for new initiatives to be developed.

Source: Drawn in part from Rebore and Walmsley 2010 and Baker College Effective Teaching and Learning Department 2004

New teachers who are in their twenties are members of the Millennial Generation, or Generation Y, and as the table illustrates, they think and function differently than older teachers do. Unlike teachers who are part of earlier generations, Generation Y teachers want to work collaboratively, desiring to solve problems and discuss issues related to teaching in groups rather than individually. Also, this new generation views change as an expected, exciting, and normal part of life, so they will look for ways to precipitate change, a tendency that is quite different from the traits of other generations. Technologically, Generation Y is the most tech-savvy and digitally connected group ever, but administrators need to remember that *connections* don't always assume *commitment,* so these new teachers need to experience satisfaction and job fulfillment through meaningful leadership and relationships. If considering the old adage "Knowledge is power" to be true, Generation Y teachers would understand the Internet to be the source of both the knowledge and the power. Because of their high reliance on and familiarity with various technologies, Generation Y teachers expect rapid responses to e-mails, but they may not be as socially intelligent as their older counterparts—even though technology makes more virtual connections, it can also encourage more isolation. They have grown educationally with a blend of entertainment and technology ("edutainment"), so multitasking and multimedia are part of their DNA. Finally, Generation Y teachers are perhaps more highly educated than their predecessors, but they may have been more pampered and protected by their parents, and that reality can create problems as Gen Yers transition into a career. These are all general characteristics of Gen Yers, or millennials, but wise educational leaders will be aware of these differences as they seek not only to recruit and hire younger teachers, but also to retain them as these novices begin to work with veteran teachers from other generations.

The implications of this chapter for educational leaders are significant ones that will require much wisdom and skill to navigate. As will be demonstrated in chapter 6, Christian schools need to consider alternate models of leadership in order for comprehensive induction and PLCs to become effective, because fostering growth among the faculty—both novice and veteran—takes time and effort. Not as difficult perhaps as "herding cats," leading multigenerational faculty members can pose a formidable challenge if everyone is not pulling in the same direction.

Feeding Our Young:
An Introduction to
Comprehensive Induction

The lips of the righteous nourish many.   —Proverbs 10:21

For educators reading this book, memories of that first year of teaching may begin to flood back. What are the emotions that come to mind? Do you remember that first classroom and that first group of students? How long did it take to feel like a "real" teacher? Were you ready to teach on that first day of school? Did you feel supported by the administration and the other teachers? If so, how did they support you? What were the mistakes made by both you as a new teacher and by the administration? Did you feel free to make mistakes and talk about them, or were you afraid you might lose your job?

This chapter serves as an introduction to *comprehensive induction*, which is "an intentional, inclusive, and sustained process, relationship, and plan through which novice teachers are mentored, acculturated, trained, assessed, and supported as contributing members of a professional learning community." This definition is lengthy so that all the important and overlapping elements of a comprehensive induction program for schools can be clearly described. Most veteran teachers and many new teachers have never experienced the benefits of a comprehensive induction program, but this chapter and the next will make the argument that an effective program will benefit teachers, administrators, and students. Instead of being the profession that "eats its young" (Halford 1998, 33), Christian schools in particular need to learn how to nourish their young teachers, nurturing them through their first few years of teaching so that novices can become effective educators. Although this chapter provides only an overview of comprehensive induction, the next chapter will give details of a sample comprehensive induction program complete with information and resources a school can use to get started.

Background of Comprehensive Induction

Many books and articles have been written about mentoring and induction, and not all writers agree on the definitions. Induction, in the opinion of some, like Leslie Huling-Austin (1990), consists of planned programs that provide "systematic and sustained assistance, specifically to beginning teachers for at least one school year (p. 536)" (Doerger 2003). Other definitions are more general: a "support, guidance and orientation program ... for beginning elementary and secondary teachers during the transition into their first teaching jobs" (Ingersoll and Kralik 2004, 1). "Phrases like 'learning the ropes' and 'eased entry' suggest that induction is about helping new teachers fit into the existing system" (Feiman-Nemser 2003, 27). Harry Wong (2002a, 52) offers a more detailed description of induction as the process of training, supporting, and retaining new teachers by

+ providing instruction in classroom-management and effective-teaching techniques,
+ reducing the difficulty of the transition into teaching, and
+ maximizing the retention rate of highly qualified teachers.

He notes that a good induction program begins before the first day of school and typically runs for two to three years.

Susan Johnson and Susan Kardos (2005) suggest several strategies for schools to develop comprehensive induction programs. Their following statements highlight some key challenges and opportunities for administrators:

+ *Treat the hiring process as the first step of induction* (11).
+ *Assign new teachers to work alongside experienced teachers* (12).
+ *Schedule time for new and veteran teachers to meet.*
+ *Provide more than one-to-one mentoring.*
+ *Develop school-based induction programs led by experienced teachers.*
+ *Organize ongoing professional development on the curriculum* (13).
+ *Encourage teacher leadership and differentiated roles.*

"All successful induction programs help new teachers establish effective classroom management procedures, routines, and instructional practices.... We must go beyond mentoring to comprehensive induction programs.... Induction includes all the activities that train and support new teachers, and it acculturates them to the mission and philosophy of their [new] school.... And the good news is that teachers stay where they feel successful, supported, and part of a [working] team" (Wong 2002a, 52). As an example, the Partners in Education (PIE) Program, an induction program jointly administered by the University of Colorado at Boulder and six neighboring school districts, has successfully used a three-part program since 1987. The three prongs of PIE are (1) intensive mentoring, (2) cohort group networking, and (3) ongoing inquiry into practice. After years of success, they conclude that "induction does indeed matter, that a meaningful induction experience has lasting effects on teacher quality and retention" (Kelley 2004, 447).

The differences between mentoring and comprehensive induction listed in table 2 demonstrate how mentoring is just a part of a complete comprehensive induction program.

Table 2. Mentoring versus comprehensive induction

Mentoring	Comprehensive induction
Focuses on survival and support	Promotes career learning and professional development
Relies on a single mentor	Provides multiple supports
Is an isolated event	Is comprehensive and is a part of lifelong professional growth
Spends limited resources	Is an investment in an extensive and continual program
Reacts to events	Acculturates a vision and aligns to standards
Is short-term (usually a year)	Is long-term, recurrent, and sustained

Source: Adapted from Wong 2004

Mentoring, however, is crucially important for a successful comprehensive induction program, and it therefore merits specific attention.

Mentoring

The following vivid metaphor captures the prospect of the mentoring process as skilled and veteran teachers invest time, energy, and wisdom into novice teachers:

> Ecologists tell us that a tree planted in a clearing of an old forest will grow more successfully than one planted in an open field. The reason, it seems, is that the roots of the forest tree are able to follow the intricate pathways created by former trees and thus embed themselves more deeply. Indeed, over time, the roots of many trees may actually graft themselves to one another, creating an interdependent mat of life hidden beneath the earth. This literally enables the stronger trees to share resources with the weaker so the whole forest becomes healthier. (Zachary 2000, xiii)

As will be demonstrated, though, the mentoring process must be viewed as a two-way street on which both the novice teachers and the veteran teachers grow and learn together.

The purpose of mentoring is to provide support, encouragement, knowledge, and feedback for novice teachers as well as provide professional development, learning, and growth for the mentor. The term *mentor* originated in Homer's *Odyssey*. When Odysseus, King of Ithaca, goes to fight in the Trojan War, he entrusts his home, his wife, and his son Telemachus to the care of Mentor, who serves as Telemachus' teacher and overseer. After the war, Telemachus, accompanied by Mentor, goes in search of his father, overcoming numerous obstacles because of Mentor's training and thus demonstrating the effectiveness of the process. Over time, the word *mentor* became synonymous with a trusted *friend*, an *advisor*, a *teacher*, a *guide*, and a *wise person*.

In school settings, a mentor is usually a veteran teacher who is linked rather informally with a new teacher in the department. The mentor is encouraged to meet with the new teacher periodically, answer questions, perhaps observe classes occasionally, help anticipate problems, and generally function as a friend. Certainly better than nothing at all, the traditional mentoring program meets some needs but leaves many unattended. Some of the common weaknesses of traditional mentoring programs include (1) no training for the mentor, (2) no formal process for choosing the mentor, (3) no compensation or other incentives for mentoring, (4) a lack of formal structures to ensure successful mentoring, and (5) a premature ending of the mentoring process.

In schools in which these weaknesses have been addressed, mentoring has proved to be an effective part of helping novice teachers grow and improve. Novice teachers interviewed by the Public Education Network reported that mentoring was "the most effective form of assistance and support in their first years" (Makkonen 2004). For this success to occur, however, systematic support in terms of administrative endorsement, stipends, release time, training for the mentor, and careful attention to the matches between mentors and novices are needed (Halford 1998, 35). The mentor and the novice must have clear and attainable goals that include accountability measures, and both need to anticipate growing professionally through the process.

Funding mentoring programs continues to be an issue, but some promising initiatives are showing good results. For example, a pilot program (funded through a federal grant) inaugurated in the 2005/2006 school year by Virginia Commonwealth University's Center for Teacher Leadership has hired twelve veteran teachers in Richmond to serve for two years as "beginning teacher advisers." These experienced educators have no regular teaching responsibilities, but they work intensively with ten to fifteen new teachers throughout the year while still earning their regular teaching salary (Kersten 2006, 9–10). A small number of larger Christian schools have also tried this approach, assigning one of the best teachers to work directly with novice teachers for a year, but this practice is rare.

Further, in a lengthy evaluation of ten mentoring programs, Richard Ingersoll and Jeffrey Kralik conclude that "assistance for new teachers—and in particular, teacher mentoring programs—[has] a positive impact on teachers and their retention" (2004, 14). Effective mentoring must go beyond just emotional support and include a strong emphasis on the development of professional accountability and (as will be discussed in chapter 5) enfold the new teachers into professional learning communities (PLCs) since comprehensive induction is the gateway for those PLCs. To that end, Cynthia Carver and Daniel Katz argue that (1) mentors must be trained and must have at their disposal a wide repertoire of effective strategies, (2) a change in expectations is needed in the teaching profession as mentors guide and instruct novice teachers, and (3) mentors will need to take on more of an assessment-oriented role as they hold themselves and their novices to high standards. "Too many induction programs are narrowly focused on providing short-term support for immediate problems rather than on ongoing commitment to teacher development (Feiman-Nemser 2000)" (Carver and Katz 2004, 450). Again, important keys to all of this teacher development are strong administrative support, time, and financing—all of which will clearly demonstrate that mentoring is a high priority.

Finally, Thomas McCann, Larry Johannessen, and Bernard Ricca summarize the research on mentoring and offer five common components of an effective mentoring program:

> (1) careful selection and training of mentors, including training in communication and peer coaching techniques; (2) attention to the expressed concerns of

beginning teachers; (3) special consideration for the inevitable exhaustion and decline that teachers experience after the first 9–10 weeks of school; (4) a program of regularly scheduled contacts between the new teacher and the mentor; and (5) assistance in acclimating the new teacher to the school community. (2005, 32)

In light of chapter 2's descriptions of Generation Y teachers, it seems wise to consider ways for novice teachers to be assigned to small groups as opposed to one-on-one mentoring if possible. First, in larger schools, administrators may consider using a veteran teacher as a mentor for the entire year, linking that teacher on a regular basis with a group of novice teachers.

Second, schools should consider a *triad approach* for all novice teachers—and this approach will work with large and small schools alike. The triad links each new teacher with at least three other educators for the year:

1. The *lead teacher*, who is the one through whom the novice will receive the most immediate help with the actual curriculum for teaching
2. The *department chair*, who oversees and assists the new teacher in other ways related to the department, including evaluating the new teacher
3. The *mentor*, who is a *nonevaluative* friend, colleague, and advisor who meets regularly with the new teacher

The mentor also observes the teaching of the new teacher, but not in a formal, evaluative way. It's crucial that the mentor be in a nonevaluative role so that the novice can be as open and honest as possible. The mentor and the novice attend monthly meetings organized by the administrative team in addition to contacting each other daily.

Finally, various administrators observe and evaluate each new teacher several times during the school year. All of these connections, along with the Teacher Induction Program for Success (TIPS) explained in the next chapter, and regular teacher-orientation meetings in August make for a successful first year of teaching.

More specifics on the roles and responsibilities of the lead teacher, the department chair, and the mentor are listed below.

Lead Teacher

The primary roles of the lead teacher are to provide curricular materials and to offer curricular oversight as well as to help the new teacher adopt a pace that will enable him or her to fulfill the curricular expectations for the whole school year.

Because not every new teacher will be assigned a lead teacher, the responsibilities delineated below can be divided (under the chair's direction) between the department chair and the mentor:

+ Providing tests, handouts, worksheets, essays, projects, PowerPoint presentations, and other materials for the new teacher's use
+ Meeting with the new teacher during the summer induction to answer questions about the curriculum
+ Meeting regularly to answer questions about the curriculum and about assessment
+ Providing suggestions for other resources (books, articles, websites)
+ Communicating regularly with the department chair and the mentor

Department Chair

The primary role of the department chair is to provide the resources necessary for the new teacher's success, to communicate the expectations of the department, and to evaluate the teacher's effectiveness in the classroom.

Specific ways in which the chair serves as a resource include the following:

+ Providing information concerning departmental policies, supplies, textbook ordering, and conference or seminar opportunities
+ Meeting with new teachers during the July or August induction meetings in order to introduce departmental policies and practices
+ Communicating departmental expectations concerning the school's philosophy of curriculum and general curricular issues
+ Giving the new teacher an updated scope and sequence, including copies of assessments used in each class to which the new teacher has been assigned
+ Observing and evaluating new teachers in the department
+ Approving final exams each semester, two weeks before exams are scheduled

+ Explaining and overseeing departmental responsibilities such as scope and sequence, AP audits, and accreditation and certification issues
+ Designating teaching assignments and providing the necessary resources and equipment to fulfill those assignments

Mentor

The primary roles of the mentor are to answer the routine questions that arise concerning the daily routines of the school, to provide a listening ear, and to help the new teacher master the craft of teaching.

Specific ways in which the mentor serves as a resource include the following:

+ Providing a sounding board for concerns, frustrations, and successes
+ Explaining the nuts and bolts of routine procedures proactively and regularly as they arise
+ Observing and discussing teaching style, classroom practice, lesson planning, grading procedures, and policies
+ Explaining responsibilities attached to new-student orientation, parent-teacher conferences, and other regularly scheduled events
+ Helping the new teacher develop a manageable professional development plan
+ Scheduling weekly meetings with the new teacher
+ Meeting with the new teacher during summer induction
+ Examining the teacher's assessments to check for adherence to the philosophy of curriculum and the level of difficulty of the assignment
+ Identifying high-quality veteran teachers to observe and to follow up those visits with discussions
+ Arranging for videotaping of the new teacher; reviewing that video together
+ Suggesting resources that address deficiencies in curriculum or struggles with classroom management
+ Working with the department chair to determine supplementary materials
+ Evaluating the final exam at least two weeks before finals begin in order to ensure the appropriateness of the test before it is passed on to the department chair for approval

Each school needs to determine the structures that work best. For smaller schools a triad approach may not be possible, so the responsibilities listed above will have to be reassigned and negotiated. It is imperative, though, that the novice teacher have support people and systems available to him or her before the beginning of the academic year, and it is most desirable that at least one of those people function in a nonevaluative way to encourage and support the novice teacher. Finding ways to provide novice teachers with (1) desirable teaching assignments that require as few preparations as possible, (2) limited or no cocurricular responsibilities for the first year, (3) mentors who are willing to learn and grow with these novice teachers, (4) the freedom to fail and experiment, and (5) numerous opportunities both to observe teaching and to be observed teaching will create a healthy environment in which comprehensive induction can be successful.

Now that comprehensive induction has been introduced, the next chapter provides specific guidelines for Christian schools to create a TIPS for all new teachers.

Teacher Induction Program for Success

If schools are using the same strategies and kids are failing, who are the slow learners?

The path to becoming a master teacher is strewn with obstacles that can delay or discourage a new teacher, or derail him or her altogether. Ideally, a candidate for teaching will receive a comprehensive and rigorous college education high in content knowledge; thorough in pedagogical, methodological, and assessment training; and replete with numerous opportunities for practice teaching in clinical pre-service experiences before certification. What follows is at least one to two years of a comprehensive induction program that accomplishes many of the purposes described in chapter 3. This proposed path assumes that the newly certified teacher is still in need of support, guidance, instruction, and supervision, along with many opportunities to grow professionally.

As noted earlier, "placing new teachers in the most challenging classrooms without comprehensive induction … is like putting newly licensed drivers in the top heat of a NASCAR race" (Alliance for Excellent Education 2004, 2). Imagine a newly graduated doctor or lawyer being thrown right into an operating room or a courtroom without first completing an internship during which he or she receives mentoring and training by seasoned veterans! But often this unrealistic type of scenario is exactly what happens in Christian schools. Despite commonly held, erroneous notions that almost anyone can teach, teaching is an extraordinarily complex and specialized profession requiring certain skills, knowledge, and dispositions—and lots of practice! Yet in most situations, a first-year teacher usually takes charge of the classroom in relative isolation from the very first day of the school year in a cruel sort of sink-or-swim ritual that has played out in schools for too long.

"The goal of a structured, comprehensive, sustained induction program is to produce effective teachers. Effective teachers are successful; students of effective teachers are successful; and, most important, successful teachers stay" (Wong 2002b, 56). A comprehensive induction program for new teachers takes time, resources, and effort, but the short- and long-term payoffs for a school—and for student learning—are significant. So how does a school get started in providing such a program? What follows are the essential components.

Acculturation Workshops

New teachers need the opportunity to experience some acculturation to their new school community before the full-faculty orientation occurs, because each school culture is unique. The specific activities and events can change on the basis of an individual school, but the Teacher Induction Program for Success (TIPS) described in table 3 demonstrates a good variety of icebreaker activities, professional development presentations, and introductions for a three-to-five-day preorientation. Note that the mentor teachers participate in only the third day of the sample schedule that follows. Note also that ideally these three days occur during the summer so new teachers have time to digest all the information and to work on their curricular materials once they have met their lead teacher, department chair, and mentor. If a summer preorientation is cost prohibitive, then these three days can take place at least a day or two before the rest of the faculty arrive for regular orientation. Providing time for acculturation to the unique community of an individual school, though, is a critical first step for the long-term success of new teachers.

The reason acculturation is so important relates to the climate (how things "feel") and culture (how things "are done") of the particular school. One author has suggested that each school possesses a unique institutional DNA, "an organizational genetic code," that must be passed on to all new teachers. The current administration and the faculty are "carriers" of that DNA, and induction allows them to reproduce it in new teachers. "Faculty members who become carriers of the organization's DNA replicate it in other faculty members as well as in the students and parents" (Keenan 2000–2001, 16–17). Each school is unique, so it's important from the beginning to help new teachers navigate these climatic and cultural waters.

The following is a sample outline of activities for a TIPS summer preorientation, which serves as the start of a larger comprehensive induction program for new teachers:

Table 3.   TIPS (Teacher Induction Program for Success)
Sample activities for a summer preorientation

Thursday, July 7	
8:30 AM	Devotions/Prayer and Introductions
9:15 AM	Group Juggle (icebreaker activity)
9:30 AM	Our Heritage—the History of Our Christian School
9:45 AM	Meet the In-house Expert: Angela Gardner—the Learning Center director on meeting special needs of students
10:15 AM	Break
10:25 AM	Mission Statement Puzzle (icebreaker activity)
10:40 AM	Neighborhood Structure—How Each Student Is Under the Guidance of at Least One Adult
11:00 AM	Meet the In-house Expert: Michael Robertson—business manager
11:20 AM	Harry Wong: "The Effective Teacher"—DVD #1
Noon	Lunch
12:45 PM	Meet the In-house Expert: Janet Dodson—coordinator for school spirit and traditions

1:15 PM	Harry Wong: "The First Days of School"—DVD #2
2:15 PM	Meet the In-house Expert: Helen Vasterling—representative of the Guidance department
2:45 PM	Mentoring Program Overview (what to expect)
3:00 PM	Dismissal

Friday, July 8	
8:30 AM	Devotions/Prayer
9:00 AM	Two Truths and a Lie (icebreaker activity)
9:15 AM	Meet the In-house Expert: Randy Ford—physical-plant director
9:25 AM	Philosophy of Curriculum (explanation and discussion)
10:15 AM	Break
10:25 AM	Most Famous Person (icebreaker activity)
10:45 AM	Harry Wong: "Discipline and Procedures"—DVD #3
Noon	Lunch
12:45 PM	Daily Schedule (explanation)
1:00 PM	Meet the In-house Expert: William Fox—technology coordinator (RenWeb School Management Software demonstrated in the computer room)
3:00 PM	Dismissal

Note: *The first two days in this scenario are followed by a weekend, so meals, outings, and other social events unique to the geographical area must be planned ahead of time. (The weekend shouldn't be overscheduled, but at least one casual event should be planned.) Information about Sunday worship options should also be provided.*

Monday, July 11 (mentor teachers included)	
8:30 AM	Devotions/Prayer
9:00 AM	RenWeb Orientation (continued, if needed)
11:00 AM	Professional Growth and Evaluation (program description)

11:15 AM	Harry Wong: "Procedures and Routines" — DVD #4
Noon	Lunch (with mentors)
12:45 PM	Meet the In-house Expert: Tom Smithson — librarian
1:00 PM	Maze Exercise (icebreaker activity)
1:30 PM	Harry Wong: "Cooperative Learning and Culture" — DVD #5
2:30 PM	Meet the In-house Expert: Steven Kim — audiovisual needs
3:00 PM	Dismissal

Monthly Meetings

Once the preorientation phase of comprehensive induction has been completed in July and all new teachers have been assigned to lead teachers, department chairs, and mentors, a plan must be implemented for the ongoing, yearlong, comprehensive program. This plan includes

+ regular supervision and evaluation visits so the new teacher receives feedback,
+ opportunities to observe master teachers in the classroom,
+ incorporation into professional learning communities (PLCs) within the school (discussed in chapter 5), and
+ opportunities to attend at-least-monthly meetings with other new teachers and all mentors.

These monthly meetings can take place either before or after school and can address topics like classroom management, parent-teacher conferences, professional growth, understanding and using assessments, curriculum issues, differentiated-instruction models, and other important subjects for new teachers. Having some light refreshments (choice of refreshments based on a survey of favorite snacks, conducted during the TIPS summer preorientation) and keeping these meetings to an hour or less will enhance productivity. If the school has purchased the Harry Wong DVD series mentioned in the "Comprehensive Induction Resources" section at the end of this chapter, one or more of the segments can be used during these monthly meetings.

Professional Development Plans

New teachers need opportunities for growth and maturity through a structured, comprehensive, and sequenced professional development plan (PDP) as they start their careers. In reality, comprehensive induction begins long before the creation of a PDP; it starts with the advertising, interviewing, and recruitment phases of the hiring process as school leaders begin the process of initiation—that is, the initiation of prospective new teachers to the school, its culture, and its personnel.

The larger context under which the role of a PDP falls is the PLC. Although PLCs will be discussed further in the next chapter, it's important to emphasize here that the professional growth of new teachers ought to be a high priority. For one thing, new teachers just graduating from teacher education programs come to their first teaching job with new knowledge and skills that can benefit veteran teachers. Second, regular supervision and feedback on teaching performance is necessary, and ideally this supervision and feedback should come from administrators, the lead teacher, the department chair (if the school appoints department chairs), the mentor, and other colleagues. Also, teachers should videotape and view their own teaching—an often uncomfortable yet extremely revealing time of learning. Third, new teachers can benefit from observing master teachers in action and then discussing teaching and learning with those masters. Fourth, within PLCs, new teachers can be included in committee work, grade-level teams, academic departments, curriculum-planning groups, and a variety of other small collegial groups. Fifth, even though historically, new teachers often get some of the less-desirable teaching assignments, schools should strongly consider assigning all new teachers to smaller classes that require limited preparations and should consider *not* assigning any cocurricular coaching or other duties for the first year—in other words doing everything possible to ensure a successful first year of professional work.

However, PDPs are not just for new teachers but for all teachers. Traditionally, professional development has consisted of in-service training days during which an outside speaker or consultant presents. Usually in-services happen this way: the school administration makes plans without consulting with the faculty, the topic for the day may or may not relate directly to specific needs of faculty, and there is no assessment or follow-up after the guest leaves. Consequently many faculty have grown cynical about professional development or in-service days because these training days seem to be irrelevant to the rest of the faculty's academic work. By establishing a PDP model for each teacher, the specific plans for professional growth can be tailored to the specific needs of faculty (in consultation with lead teachers, department chairs, grade-level chairs, mentors, principals, and deans). The PDP itself should align to the mission, purpose, and educational objectives of the school, focusing teachers on the following:

+ *The previous year's formative and summative evaluations*: These evaluations guide the formation of the PDP since these documents include improvement-needed areas. Teachers should review the previous year's formative and summative evaluations and begin to consider options for their PDP before they consult with an administrator, a mentor, or a peer.

+ *Specific plans*: Teachers should submit specific plans (complete with action steps and target dates) for their professional growth objectives for the year. Each teacher can complete the PDP either individually or with a small group. Ideas for PDP activities may include attending or presenting at a conference (and for either, reporting back to the whole faculty); conducting action research on a particular topic; videotaping and observing classes of other teachers; completing graduate work; reading books and discussing them among colleagues; mentoring a new teacher for the year; or formulating and proposing a new curriculum, class, or program for the school. The goal, of course, is that the yearly PDP activities clearly apply to the needs of the individual teacher.

+ *PDP approval and progress reports*: Teachers should obtain approval from the appropriate administrator for their completed PDP and should submit progress reports periodically throughout the year. The administrator should include a short PDP-completion report as part of the yearly summative evaluation of each teacher.

More Components That Promote Teacher Induction

When building or renovating buildings, schools can consider creating common work spaces for teachers as another innovative way to encourage professional growth, strong relationships, and collaborative groups. In contrast to traditional work-space models that isolate teachers in their own classrooms, common work spaces encourage teachers to interact and form collegial communities that foster learning. New teachers can do common planning with veteran teachers while at the same time benefiting from the more informal, spontaneous conversations that occur every day. In settings like this, induction becomes "not only ... a set of separate interventions but also ... a set of structural conditions" (Shank 2005, 19).

In addition to common work spaces, schools can consider assigning new teachers to a triad of mentors as described in the previous chapter: a lead teacher, a department head, and a formal mentor. This triad approach along with various administrative supports and small groups will go a long way in helping new teachers grow and succeed professionally.

Finally, schools can consider producing personnel directories that include job descriptions as well as a glossary of the unique events, traditions, organizations, and nomenclature used in the school. All of these plans will enable schools to become true learning communities.

Crucial factors in all of this, of course, are strong board and administration support and encouragement coupled with the time, resources, and space to provide comprehensive induction. One study group credited the administrative support they received through induction with "setting the right mix of challenge and support that enables schools to become joyful, creative, productive places" (Williams 2003, 74).

In fact, an important emphasis for teacher- and administrator-preparation programs should be to promote effective educational leadership training that strongly endorses comprehensive induction within graduate training. Such an emphasis trains teachers to expect administrative support and trains administrators to strongly encourage comprehensive induction.

Successful Comprehensive Induction Programs

Two particular programs show encouraging promise for the success of comprehensive induction programs. The first is the Teacher Induction Program at Northern Arizona University's College of Education (TIP @ NAU). Partially funded through the U.S. Department of Education, the TIP @ NAU employs full-time mentors to work with 268 new teachers in five school districts. Although the program is new, it is already showing promising results in the areas of teacher retention, teaching practice, and student achievement (Horn et al. 2006). The second program is the Alabama Teacher Training and Induction

Network (ATTAIN) at the University of Alabama–Birmingham. ATTAIN works with teacher education graduates for five years after graduation to assist with various professional development issues common to new teachers.

"For first year teachers, then, the induction year can be crucial to their decision to continue teaching.… Induction programs, therefore, should not only provide assistance with technical educational issues, they should also provide the new teacher with opportunities to begin to understand the school's culture and the effect of that culture on the school's climate" (Doerger 2003). Citing a Michigan Education Association (2000) brochure, Sharon Feiman-Nemser says that there is "an emerging consensus among U.S. educators and policymakers that the retention of new teachers depends on effective mentors and induction programs" (2003, 25).

Comprehensive Induction Resources

In addition to the works cited in the further-reading and reference lists at the end of the book, here are some recommended comprehensive induction resources and short descriptions:

The Effective Teacher DVD series by Harry K. Wong (Mountain View, CA: Harry K. Wong Publications, 2005)
This 8-DVD workshop series includes titles such as "The First Days of School" and "Procedures and Routines." It is an excellent resource for use in TIPS and throughout the year.

Effective Teacher Induction and Mentoring: Assessing the Evidence by Michael Strong (New York: Teachers College Press, 2009)
As the name implies, this book is a comprehensive and up-to-date review of all recent research related to induction and mentoring programs. The author argues that even though much more research needs to be done the early evidence shows that these programs promote retention.

Leading the Teacher Induction and Mentoring Program, second edition, by Barry W. Sweeny (Thousand Oaks, CA: Corwin Press, 2008)
This is a book designed specifically for those who are leading new-teacher programs in their school. Sweeny offers step-by-step instructions, diagrams, and reproducible materials.

"Links to Web-Based Teaching Induction Quality Resources," a Web page of ATTAIN: www.ed.uab.edu/attain/resources.html
This ATTAIN Web page links to other websites containing information about comprehensive induction for teachers.

The Mentoring Year: A Step-by-Step Program for Professional Development **by Susan Udelhofen and Kathy Larson (Thousand Oaks, CA: Corwin Press, 2003)**
As the name implies, this is a book loaded with checklists, tools, templates, rubrics, surveys, and a variety of other usable materials to establish a mentoring program for new teachers.

New Teacher Induction: How to Train, Support, and Retain New Teachers **by Annette L. Breaux and Harry K. Wong (Mountain View, CA: Harry K. Wong Publications, 2003)**
This is a how-to book that gives details about dozens of induction programs from around the country. It includes not only the arguments for induction but also many reproducible materials.

Ready for Anything: Supporting New Teachers for Success **by Lynn F. Howard (Englewood, CO: Advanced Learning Press, 2006)**
This is a ready-made, yearlong seminar book that can be used with new teachers. It includes sample agendas, strategies, checklists, and other practical advice for teacher induction.

Professional Learning Communities in Christian Schools

He who walks with the wise grows wise.   —Proverbs 13:20

As mentioned earlier, the need for a seamless relationship from pre-service clinical practice to comprehensive induction to professional learning communities (PLCs) is the central argument of this book, and this relationship is demonstrated by the diagram below:

Fig. 1. A seamless relationship.

45

Introduction: A Narrative from the Front Lines

The words *accreditation visit* are often met with moans and groans by teachers and administrators alike. All the data collection, report writing, document revisions, and other preparations can be time-consuming and daunting, and some people view them as unnecessary busywork.

When carried out properly, though, accreditation can be a helpful growth process for a school. In my twenty-three years of work at a Christian school, the seven-year reaccreditation process was a clear impetus for almost every significant change and improvement in the school. When outside observers visited and made their recommendations, we always used their suggestions to initiate needed changes. One example relates to the school's philosophy of curriculum.

In 1996, the visiting team for our school listed the following as one of their major recommendations: the school should "carefully and comprehensively evaluate its curriculum." Only six words, but an enormous task.

Our school was founded in 1976, and those early years flew by without much attention given to the careful development of a biblical philosophy of curriculum. For the most part, individual courses and departments were cobbled together in fits and starts, but the overall coherence was lacking—a fact the visiting reaccreditation team correctly identified as an area needing improvement. We knew that it is important for Christian schools to build their curriculum "from the bottom up" as they begin with the authority of the Bible, but the tyranny of the urgent prevailed. The fact is, when Christian schools simply imitate what non-Christian schools do, they open themselves up to "the danger of inviting the Trojan horse into the City of God" (Oppewal 1985, 9).

Even though none of us had ever heard of professional learning communities—the term "first appeared in the published scholarly literature in 1992 (Cuban 1992, McLaughlin 1992)" (Louis 2006, 478)—we formed a group of ten teachers and administrators to create our school's philosophy of curriculum so that the whole curriculum could be assessed through that filter. Our intentionally cross-discipline team included both the middle- and high-school principals. The chair of our curriculum committee was a science teacher, and he carefully selected a number of chapters and articles from a variety of authors on the subject, creating a two-inch-thick binder of readings in preparation for our meetings. The head of school provided money for stipends and lunches, allowed time for us to meet in the summer, and offered other support and encouragement; and so we set out for a week of grappling, debating, learning, and discovering—one of the most rewarding times of professional learning that many of us had ever experienced.

We began with an inverted-pyramid approach:

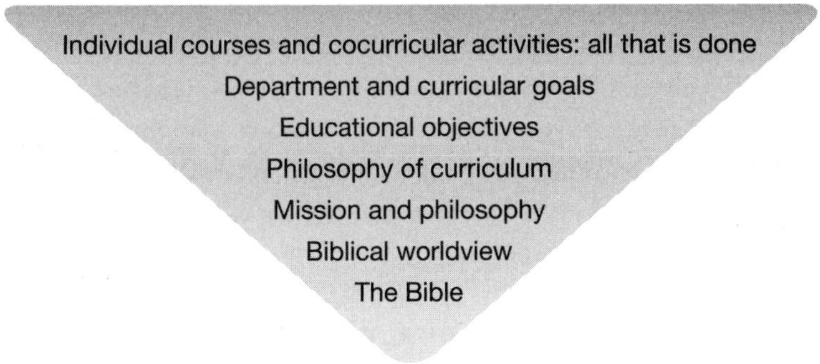

Individual courses and cocurricular activities: all that is done
Department and curricular goals
Educational objectives
Philosophy of curriculum
Mission and philosophy
Biblical worldview
The Bible

Fig. 2. The pyramid of curriculum planning.

Since the middle piece was missing, it was our committee's task to create a philosophy of curriculum. We confidently believed that some of the curricular and cocurricular activities at our school were good, but it was also apparent that others were merely imitative of secular models. What we needed was a biblically based philosophy of curriculum to guide our thinking and planning.

Originally, the committee had hoped not only to produce a philosophy-of-curriculum statement, but also to use that document to evaluate the school's curriculum—a rather ambitious agenda for five days. Instead, the committee spent the week producing a twelve-page document divided into these categories: epistemology (nature of knowledge), anthropology (nature of the learner), motivation, and pedagogy. Each of these main areas is subdivided into key principles under which are a series of questions. For example, the following principle falls under the anthropology category:

Principle 1: The learner bears God's image. Therefore, the learner is

A. Creative: Genesis 2:19, Genesis 1:25–26

Questions to Consider:

1. Do my evaluative tools address only one learning style?
2. Do I recognize my students' creativity in designing curriculum?
3. Is there only one right answer or one right way to do things in my class? (Westminster Christian Academy 1997)

As a temporary PLC, our curriculum committee who met that summer proved to be transformative. Several participants abandoned previous lesson plans, assignments, and other strategies to pursue curriculum development, using the guidance of this new document. Unfortunately those transformative effects did not translate to the rest of the faculty because they had not participated in the extensive readings and discussions; also, this PLC did not continue to meet—both negative realities that will be discussed later. Yet that momentous week in July 1997 serves as an excellent example of how PLCs can strengthen Christian schooling.

Professional Learning Communities Defined

The twentieth-century paradigm of staff development primarily through in-service is giving way to a new structure that encourages relationships, community building, collaboration, and both student and teacher learning. *Professional learning communities* are "groups of educators intentionally committed to continual learning for themselves and students through shared values, reflection, and dialogue, all under the guidance of the school's mission." Ann Lieberman and Lynne Miller argue that PLCs can exist within a school, across disciplines and grade levels, across school and district lines, and even electronically across state lines (2008, 2). Learning communities can include professional networks, study groups, research collaboratives, video conferencing, and other combinations.

The older models of staff development assumed that the teacher was present mainly to transmit knowledge to students, and this work was often done incompletely and in relative isolation. Training models and curriculum designs (curriculum guides, test booklets, packets of handouts and overheads—one-size-fits-all and "idiot proof") were written by the "experts" at national offices or universities and passed down to classroom teachers. By contrast, a PLC emphasizes a collective repertoire of teaching practice, collegiality, clear links between teaching and learning, a shared knowledge base, collaborative goals and purposes, support for newcomers and veterans alike, a recognition that teaching is more an art than a science, and the insistence that judgments of success are based on student demonstrations of learning (Lieberman and Miller 2008, 33).

Dissecting the definition above by looking more carefully at each of its parts is instructive.

Educators

For PLCs to function effectively, there must be logical and purposeful reasons for them to exist, such as all seventh-grade teachers' working together as a team; all high school English teachers' planning and constructing the curriculum together; the upper-elementary teachers' collaborating to ensure that subjects are taught in a systematic, coherent, and progressive way; or interdisciplinary groups' being tasked with specific jobs (like the curriculum committee described in the introduction of this chapter). The group size and constitution will vary, but making sure that the groups consist of all the right people is important. A science teacher, not an administrator, led the curriculum committee described earlier; his leadership underscores the fact that learning communities involve a community of leaders.

Intentional Commitment

PLCs are not quick fixes for school problems. Most of the literature says it takes years for a community to form, work through relationship issues, focus on specific issues related to learning, and begin to function well together as a team—a reality that forms another argument for comprehensive induction programs, which help avoid a revolving door of new teachers. This lengthy process calls for high levels of patience and commitment. Intentionality means that specific plans are put into place for space, time, resources, and support in order for PLCs to be successful, because "most schools' schedules are not designed to encourage collegial interaction" (Roy and Hord 2006, 495). The need for intentionality implies that if PLCs aren't a priority, they simply won't happen.

Continual Learning

The need for continual learning is at the heart of every PLC. The focus is on learning for both students and teachers, and this shared focus probably demands a profound cultural shift in thinking for most schools. "Thus, the essential purpose of the PLC is staff learning for increasing students' successful learning" (Roy and Hord 2006, 494). The good news is that research shows that student learning increases when PLCs are in place. PLCs use assessment and data to determine whether students are learning and then create specific plans for improvement. "The ultimate question is whether learning communities make a difference in student achievement" (Mitchell and Sackney 2006, 629), and according to the data, they do.

Shared Values

Most of the literature on PLCs talks at length about how important it is for teachers and administrators to agree on basic values and beliefs, suggesting that some of the more difficult "negotiations" in relationships occur at this point. PLCs in Christian schools have a decided advantage in that these basic values and beliefs are rooted in the authority of Scripture. To be sure, theological and personal differences can produce tensions and disagreements, but Christian school personnel have more to agree on than to disagree on, a factor that makes the development of a Christian school PLC that much easier.

Reflection

The seminal work of Donald Schön (1987), *Educating the Reflective Practitioner: Toward a New Design for Teaching and Learning in the Professions*, is one of many sources arguing that professionals need to learn the skill of reflective practice in order to better understand *what* they are doing and *why*. "Schools should seek to lead not only in learning, but also in reflecting on and about learning.... In schools students should be taught to understand and to reflect critically on what they are doing (Bowers 1987, 144) ... [in order] to act purposefully" (Stronks and Blomberg 1993, 172). Parker Palmer in *The Courage to Teach: Exploring the Inner Landscape of a Teacher's Life* reminds us that good teaching can't be reduced simply to technique (1998, 63). He writes to encourage teachers to reflect on their teaching and the "inner landscape" of their lives to create more-meaningful communities of learners in our schools. John Dewey encouraged reflection by teachers who saw their practice as experimental; reflection is necessary to evaluate and assess what is happening in the classroom (Schön 1987, 311–12). As Socrates observed centuries ago, "The unexamined life is not worth living."

"Reflection, I believe, is indispensable if teachers are to connect their educational philosophy ... with what they do in the classroom." Reflection is "a rich, multi-faceted process, and hence a practice ... a way of being ... a habit" and a means "to advance in wisdom, to journey with the Lord on the road of sanctification" (Van Dyk 2001, 47). Citing Thomas Groome (1980), John Van Dyk notes that critical reflection "is an activity in which one calls upon (1) critical reason to evaluate the present, (2) critical memory to uncover the past in the present, and (3) creative imagination to envision the future in the present (p. 185)" (2001, 48). The reflective practitioner, then, attempts to stand back from his or her teaching in order to analyze, assess, make changes, try something new, and reflect again. It must be purposely planned for and developed into a habit, a way of life, as educators learn to think, consider, evaluate, discern, and judge. Reflective practice is both an individual and communal activity as teachers and administrators consider practice, philosophy, and theory; it can actually encourage experimentation and risk taking. The assumption is that a gap exists between what Christian educators believe and know and what they actually practice in the classroom, so reflective practice can be an effective bridge for that gap.

Dialogue

A PLC must be characterized by a collaborative and collegial work culture, by commitment to the difficult and time-consuming teamwork that facilitates success in learning. In many schools teachers and administrators must learn to share and discover together. Citing Casey Stengel's famous quip "Getting good players is easy. Getting 'em to play together is the hard part," Roland Barth argues that collegiality is the best indicator of a successful PLC. Are "educators talking with one another about practice,... sharing their craft knowledge,... observing one another,... and rooting for one another's success" (2006, 11)?

Mission

Without exception, all curricular and cocurricular decisions are made in light of the school mission statement. A mission statement is a brief (often just one or two sentences) description of what the school seeks to accomplish through its educational program. A mission statement is different from a vision statement; the former describes the purpose of the school, the latter where the school plans to go in the future. "A mission statement is a terse, clear statement of purpose. It comes from answering the question: What do we expect students to be like when they finish the course? It focuses everybody's attention on the main thing" (Vander Ark 2000, 18). A PLC needs a compelling and settled vision rooted in the school's mission.

A Brief History of Administration, Leadership, and Professional Development

In the early part of the twentieth century, Frederick Taylor helped popularize an approach to school administration, an approach that emphasized efficiency, control, centralization, and standardization. Known as "scientific management," Taylor's views systematized schools and led to top-down management, bureaucracy, and a one-size-fits-all approach to schooling, what Raymond Callahan graphically describes as the "cult of efficiency" (1962, 2, 19). The effects of scientific management are still evident in many schools.

In the 1920s, innovators like social worker Mary Parker Follett (known for her book *Creative Experience*, 1924) and business executive Chester Barnard (*The Functions of the Executive*, 1938) began to focus on the human side of workers, arguing that administration is more an art than a science. Human dignity and respect were important to maintain, so communication, satisfaction, and internal motivation gave rise to what became known as the human-relations approach. Other contributors who shaped school administration include Talcott Parsons (functionalism and social equilibrium, 1937), Herbert Simon (*Administrative Behavior*, 1947), Abraham Maslow (Hierarchy of Needs model, *Motivation and Personality*, 1954), Jacob Getzels and Egon Guba (model of social systems, 1957), Douglas McGregor (theories x and y of human motivation, 1960s), and James Burns (transformational leadership, 1978). More recently, Thomas Sergiovanni, Richard DuFour, Shirley Hord, and Peter Senge stress learning organizations, shared moral leadership, and the importance of building community in schools. In a real sense, PLCs have roots in John Dewey's laboratory model for schools, in which teachers are actively engaged in research, learning, and collective inquiry. This brief history relates directly to professional development because this field is beginning to shift from a bureaucratic, efficient, and streamlined approach to teacher learning to the current perspectives on PLCs.

Components of a Professional Learning Community

Consider the following components vital to the success of any PLC.

Context

One of the first assumptions of a PLC is that the context matters: "No two professional learning communities are the same" (Lieberman and Miller 2008, 12). Pam Grossman, Sam Wineburg, and Stephen Woolworth have proposed a model for studying the way teacher communities form and grow. Their model was created on the basis of a two-and-a-half-year project that brought together twenty-four teachers from an urban high school to work on an interdisciplinary humanities curriculum. Here are four benchmarks of community growth that resulted from these authors' observations and study (2001):

1. *Formation of group identity*—that the group is enriched by multiple perspectives and that interactional norms are established
2. *Navigating of fault lines*—that the group should expect differences and conflict but learn to relate to one another with openness, respect, and honesty
3. *Negotiating of the essential tension*—that teacher learning and student learning are connected
4. *Communal responsibility for individual growth*—that the group should be committed to one another in trusting and accountable relationships

Learning, then—for teachers and students alike—is understood not just as an individual cognitive process but also as the result of social interactions (Lieberman and Miller 2008, 13). "As iron sharpens iron, so one man sharpens another" (Proverbs 27:17).

Learning

Learning must be at the heart of every PLC. "One staff developer said, 'One of the key moments occurred when our teachers moved from training to doing.... Once teachers began to "work on the work," their questions became richer and more insightful'" (Many and King 2008, 29; ellipses in original). "Professional learning communities shift their primary purpose ... from a focus on teaching to a focus on learning. This shift is seismic" (Eaker and Keating 2008, 15).

The ongoing task of PLCs in schools is the intentional commitment to regularly and frequently meet to learn as a staff on the basis of "deep exploration of student data to identify the needs of students and reflection on the extent to which the staff's work is producing the results intended" (Hord 2008, 12). An important conviction in this regard is that "best practices" are often not "out there," but located "in here," right in your own school (Lieberman and Miller 2008, 22): "Job-embedded learning opportunities often assume that expertise is internally located" (Wei et al. 2009, 9).

Collegiality

Lieberman and Miller draw a sharp distinction between congeniality and collegiality. Congenial relationships, though amiable and compatible, often suppress conflict and exist as only "pseudo-communities" that encourage "individualism, isolation, and privacy." By comparison genuine collegiality in a PLC demonstrates the following: bonds of trust, reflection, honest feedback, disagreements, responsibility, and problem solving—all in a context of sustained relationships and open dialogue (2008, 18–19), "what Little and Horn [2007] call 'consequential conversations'" (20). As these trusting, respectful, and open bonds grow within a school, teachers and administrators begin to sense a communal diligence for their own learning as well as the success and learning of all students. "When levels of collegiality are high, when teachers behave like members of a community of practice, when teachers feel morally obligated to meet their commitments to each other and to the school's purposes, and when teachers are committed to working together to do what is best for students, collective responsibility is high" (Sergiovanni 2005, 135). In a Christian school the need for transparent and vulnerable relationships is acute.

Shared Leadership

Shared leadership is an indispensable part of a successful PLC. This concept touches on the notion of professionalism, that all teachers bring knowledge, skills, and dispositions that can generate new learning and understanding given a supportive governance environment. "The principal is key for the initiation and development of any new element in the school, but the sharing prin-

cipal soon develops the leadership potential of the staff and becomes the collaborating 'guide on the side' rather than the 'sage on the stage'" (Hord 2008,
12). For most schools this will involve not just a structural but cultural shift
in how things are done. Part of this cultural change calls for a shift of focus
from teaching to students and for a shared leadership model in which power,
authority, and decision making are distributed. The old paradigm that "teachers teach, students learn, and administrators manage is completely altered....
[There is] no longer a hierarchy of who knows more than someone else, but
rather the need for everyone to contribute" (Kleine-Kracht 1993, 393).

Leadership in this sense is reflective of the words of Jesus to James and John,
who requested to sit at the right and left hand of Jesus in His kingdom: "Not
so with you. Instead, whoever wants to become great among you must be your
servant, and whoever wants to be first must be slave of all. For even the Son of
Man did not come to be served, but to serve, and to give his life as a ransom
for many" (Mark 10:43–45). "Though school leaders may be in charge, the
best of them are aware that often the teachers they supervise know more
about what needs to be done and how to do it than they do.... In covenantal
communities the purpose of leadership is to create a shared followership.
Leaders in covenantal communities function as head followers" (Sergiovanni
2000, 166–67). Sergiovanni and DuFour stress that clarity is a fundamental attribute of successful leadership, and it is the chief task of the leader to
ensure that the school stays true to its mission.

DuFour advocates a "loose and tight" leadership approach to educational leadership for PLCs. A "bottom-up approach" style doesn't work, he argues, and
an autocratic approach is too confining. Instead he advocates what Richard
Elmore (2004) calls "reciprocal accountability": educational leaders provide
both pressure and support for teachers to learn, grow, and make decisions. In
the teamwork needed for PLCs, leaders must walk a tightrope between par-
ticipating on the field and cheering in the bleachers. At times, this means that
leaders have to get out of the way and let the learning community function;
at other times, the leader needs to be the chief contributor; and at times, the
leader "must be prepared to insist those within their organizations heed, not
ignore, clear evidence of the best, most promising strategies for accomplishing
its purpose and priorities" (DuFour 2007a). "It is the leader's responsibility to

be outraged when empowerment is abused and when purposes are ignored. Moreover, all members of the school community are obligated to show outrage when the standard falls" (Sergiovanni 1992, 130). In all of these examples, Christian educators need to aggressively pursue reconciled and loving relationships with one another as a community of grace (see the chapter by Bruce Hekman [2007] on the topic of grace in *Schools as Communities: Educational Leadership, Relationships, and the Eternal Value of Christian Schooling*).

PLCs could prove to be real godsends for Christian schools in another way too. Currently, teachers perceive that they have very little input on major schoolwide decisions involving things like curriculum, scheduling, discipline, hiring, and the budget while "the principal continues to accumulate an inordinate number of responsibilities" (Moller 2006, 520–21). If ever the phrase *a win-win situation* applies, it is when it refers to the leadership demands of a PLC as teachers gain significant professional responsibilities and administrators realize they are relieved of some of the irrational superhuman expectations that have contributed to the current shortage of principals.

Collaboration

Schools as communities of professionals in which teachers and students alike are learning must be characterized by collaboration:

> It is not likely that we will be successful in transforming our classrooms into communities ... unless we are able to transform our schools similarly. Few axioms are more fundamental than the one that acknowledges the link between what happens to teachers and what happens to students. Inquiring classrooms, for example, are not likely to flourish in schools where inquiry among teachers is discouraged. A commitment to problem solving is difficult to instill in students who are taught by teachers for whom problem solving is not allowed. Where there is little discourse among teachers, discourse among students will be harder to promote and maintain. And the idea of making classrooms into learning communities for students will remain more rhetoric than real unless schools become learning communities for teachers too (Sergiovanni 1996, 139).

This communal approach is reflective of biblical principles: "Plans fail for lack of counsel, but with many advisers they succeed.... Make plans by seeking advice" (Proverbs 15:22, 20:18). Collaboration among Christian educators must begin in individual hearts fueled by humility, covered in prayer, and dependent on the Lord for the ability to extend forgiveness and mercy.

Reflective Practice

Important for a successful PLC is reflective practice, the capacity to be a self-conscious knowledge worker. Schön describes two types of reflective practice: (1) "reflection-in-action" ("thinking on your feet" [1983, 54]) and (2) "reflection-on-action" (analyzing things after the fact [276–78]), both of which help teachers understand, make predictions, plan for new courses, and make sense of learning. "Schön (1983) emphasized that reflective practice is not unidirectional and that professional knowledge does not flow from the expert to student. In his view, 'The movement of learning is as much from periphery to periphery, or from periphery to centre, as from centre to periphery' rather than being limited to 'the nexus of official policies at the centre' (p. 165)" (Lieberman and Miller 2008, 21).

Jesus tells an intriguing story in the midst of a discussion with the chief priests and the elders regarding His own authority: "There was a man who had two sons. He went to the first and said, 'Son, go and work today in the vineyard.' 'I will not,' he answered, but later he changed his mind and went. Then the father went to the other son and said the same thing. He answered, 'I will, sir,' but he did not go. Which of the two did what his father wanted?" (Matthew 21:28–31). After the Jewish leaders answer that the first son did the right thing, Jesus goes on to draw a contrast between the "tax collectors and prostitutes," who initially say no but later repent, and the religious leaders, who say yes but then don't obey. Jesus seems to be saying that correct belief (*orthodoxy*) and correct actions (*orthopraxy*)[1] are both needed—that we need to both "*say yes* and *do yes*" (Nabors 2009). The point here is that schools and educators will always have a gap between what they believe and what they do, and reflective practice is an effective way to address those disparities.

Van Dyk (2001, 54–55) suggests the following as conditions that must exist in order for reflective practice to flourish:
1. Schools must "create more reflection time for teachers, clarify and specify mission statements, and provide effective reflection-building leadership."

2. There must be regular "collegial and reciprocal talk" in schools.
3. Administratively, educational leaders need to "provide a positive, encouraging, collegial, and empowering setting" for teachers and "establish an atmosphere of confidence that reflection can lead to better (more normative) Christian education."
4. Reflective practice must be seen positively as an invitation, not a requirement; yet all involved must be held accountable.
5. "In-service on reflection makes sense only if the school's culture is reflective and if the staff development program is ongoing."

Words of Caution

At this point you may be genuinely excited about the prospect of PLCs emerging in your school, but caution is needed regarding issues surrounding these three words: *change, time,* and *systems.*

Change

First, change is always a difficult task not only for individuals but especially for schools. By nature we tend to feel more comfortable with the status quo (ruts, routines, familiar places), but the promise of PLCs is systemic change for the school. "Hosts of researchers, however, have concluded that substantive change inevitably creates discomfort and dissonance as people are asked to act in new ways" (DuFour 2007b). Michael Fullan (2008), though, has guided schools and school systems through transformations for decades, and he offers administrators six secrets for change:

1. *Love your employees*—create the conditions for teachers to succeed by helping all employees find meaning, increase their skills, and reach personal and professional satisfaction as their own goals and the goals of the institution are reached (25).
2. *Connect peers with purpose*—positive purposeful peer interaction is the goal. "Leaders have to provide direction, create the conditions for effective peer interaction, and intervene along the way when things are not working as well as they could" (49).
3. *Capacity building prevails*—leaders must invest in the continual development of individual and collaborative efficacy. First, hire and cultivate talented people, and then make sure these people are integrated into learning communities. The sum is always greater than the individual parts (13, 63).

4. *Learning is the work*—Citing Elmore (2004), Fullan notes that "there is almost no opportunity for teachers to engage in continuous and substantial learning about their practice in the setting in which they actually work, observing and being observed by their colleagues in their own classrooms.... (p. 127)" (86).

5. *Transparency rules*—schools must engage in ongoing assessment, clear and continuous display of results, and decisions made for improvement. This transparency relates to addressing problems as well as sharing strategies for success (14, 95).

6. *Systems learn*—the school can learn through the synergy of the first five secrets to unleash two dominant change forces: knowledge and commitment. "Secret Six entails grappling with system complexities, taking action, and then learning from the experiences—all while engaging other leaders" (14, 119).

Time

Second, Fullan, DuFour, and Hord emphasize that the development of an effective PLC takes time, structures, and effort. It's not a quick fix for problems, nor the latest educational fad. When designed and implemented correctly, though, a PLC can transform teaching, learning, even the whole school; but it won't happen overnight, so patience, determination, and perseverance are key. The siren call of superficiality must be resisted. "Professional learning communities are in fact about establishing lasting new collaborative cultures. Collaborative cultures are ones that focus on building the capacity for continuous improvement and are intended to be a new way of working and learning. They are meant to be enduring capacities, not just another program innovation" (Fullan 2006, 2). The reality, however, is that teachers and leaders must be committed to PLCs for the long haul, anticipating that there will be progress and failure along the way. For starters, a school can take a long and deep look at its current use of time and space, looking for ways to make meaningful changes, perhaps even restructuring the entire school day and week.

As Jim Collins observes in regard to breakthrough moments in companies: "*There was no miracle moment....* Although it may have looked like a single-stroke breakthrough ..., it was anything but that.... Rather, it was a quiet, deliberate process of figuring out what needed to be done to create the best future results and then simply taking those steps, one after the other, turn by turn of the flywheel. After pushing on that flywheel in a consistent direction over an extended period of time, they'd inevitably hit a point of breakthrough" (2001, 169).

Related to time and change is the reality that at times schools will take two steps forward and then one step back: "One of our most consistent findings and understandings about the change process in education is that *all* successful schools experience 'implementation dips'.... The implementation dip is literally a dip in performance and confidence as one encounters an innovation that requires new skills and new understandings.... Leaders who understand the implementation dip know that people are experiencing two kinds of problems ... the social-psychological fear of change, and the lack of technical know-how or skills to make the change work" (Fullan 2001, 40–41). Knowing that teachers will probably feel anxious, discouraged, confused, or overwhelmed, wise leaders will be prepared to encourage, support, and remain consistent throughout since "developing a community of practice may be the single most important way to improve a school" (Sergiovanni 2000, 139).

Systems

Third, perhaps PLCs are best understood in light of the systems approach of Peter Senge and his coauthors (2000). Senge, an organizational-learning professor at MIT, wrote *The Fifth Discipline: The Art and Practice of the Learning Organization* (New York: Doubleday/Currency), which was published in 1990. Later, he applied his ideas specifically to schools in *Schools That Learn: A Fifth Discipline Fieldbook for Educators, Parents, and Everyone Who Cares About Education*, and in that book, he and his coauthors outline the five disciplines needed for a learning community to exist:

1. *Personal mastery*—a school needs educators who are committed to lifelong learning. It is no longer adequate to simply focus on student learning. A school cannot grow if its individual members are stagnant (59–65).

2. *Mental models*—deeply held assumptions and generalizations (what might be called a worldview) are possessed by these individuals mentioned above. Senge warns of one danger that mental models present: they can be barriers to new learning (66–70), a warning similar to the

one Rick Ostrander issues in *Why College Matters to God: Academic Faithfulness and Christian Higher Education:* "To develop a mature Christian worldview, however, you will need to be willing to use more pencil" (2009, 26).

3. *Shared vision*—rooted in the mission of the school, the shared vision is a collaboratively created image of where the community is going. Shared visions allow for enthusiasm, experimentation, and creativity (71–72).

4. *Team learning*—this term refers to the structures, time, dialogue, and discussion that lead to new learning and understandings. The sum is indeed greater than the individual parts (73–76).

5. *Systems thinking*—understanding the organic nature of the school, educators look for the patterns that exist, appreciate how change in one part affects the others, and learn to focus on the whole rather than the individual parts (77–92).

The perspective noted in the above list reinforces the idea that a PLC is not a short-term solution for particular problems but rather a culturally different approach to learning and schooling. "From a systems perspective the task is not to change teachers but to help them want to change, thereby eliminating the natural pushback against change processes" (Wells and Keane 2008, 26). Citing the work of several other authors, Laura Servage argues for a "transformative learning theory" in which teachers come to new understandings about learning as paradigmatic assumptions are questioned and a "fundamental reordering of social relations and practices (Brookfield 2003, p. 142)" is pursued (2008, 66).

Organizational-learning theory assumes that learning takes place best in groups, so for schools, this means having groups of teachers gather together regularly to discuss, share, dialogue, and critique in order to create a capacity-building knowledge. "Isolating teachers in individual classrooms, departments, and grade level configurations militates against the efficient or effective sharing of individually held knowledge." Instead, "small group planning periods, regular faculty meetings devoted to discussion, and frequent lateral communication networks provide an organizational design for acquiring information (Cohen 1991)" (Louis 2006, 481) and for forming the required authentic and trusting relationships.

Educators must remember that a move toward PLCs is truly a major cultural transformation:

+ From teaching to learning
+ From isolation to collaboration
+ From coverage of material to demonstrated proficiency

Granted, these are major shifts, but here are some encouraging words regarding the resulting benefits certainly worth the time and effort:

> We have known for decades that students benefit when the teachers in their schools work in collaborative teams (Little 1990), establish a guaranteed and viable curriculum to ensure all students have access to the same knowledge and skills (Marzano 2003), monitor student learning on a frequent and timely basis (Lezotte 1997), use formative assessments to identify students who need additional support for learning (Reeves 2006), and demonstrate high expectations for student achievement through a collective commitment to help all students learn (Brophy and Good 2002). These concepts represent more than "ideas worth considering": they continue to represent best practices for meeting the needs of all students. (DuFour 2007b)

Getting Started

PLCs need administrative initiation, support, encouragement, and structures in order to be successful. Sergiovanni (1992, 74) lists six practices for educational leaders to embody for providing purposeful, moral leadership:

1. *Say it*—"define the core values" and work to clearly communicate them.
2. *Model it*—live by those core values in your own leadership.
3. *Organize for it*—ensure that these core values guide the decision making, the procedures, and the practices (for a PLC).
4. *Support it*—prioritize resources toward these core values; "the most important things get cut last."
5. *Enforce it*—make sure that core values are evident (in a PLC) and "commend practices that exemplify the core values."
6. *Express outrage*—verbalize "when practices violate the core values."

What are some of the structures and supports that need to be in place to start a PLC?

+ Regular meeting times during the school day
+ The rotation of roles and responsibilities within the group

- Training as needed for group work, assessment, use of research data
- A prepared agenda for each meeting
- A set of norms and expectations generated by the group
- The building of trust, respect, collegiality, openness—working toward authentic participation by all
- Brainstorming as a group for problems and questions of common interest
- Looking for connections between the PLC, learning, and teaching

What follows are some questions that could be used in the early stages of planning for a PLC or within an already-established community:

- Are we sure of the knowledge and the skills each student is expected to gain through this course?
- What assessment plans are in place to help us know whether students have acquired this knowledge and these skills?
- Are our assessments regularly scheduled (formative), and do they occur at the end of a grade level or a school level (summative)?
- What plans do we have in place for when we discover that students are not acquiring the knowledge and the skills we think they should be acquiring?
- How do we use the data gained from formative and summative assessments to effect change in our teaching?
- Do we really believe that all our students can learn and can achieve success?
- What would it look like in our school if we genuinely embraced the changes from teaching to learning, from isolation to collaboration, from coverage to proficiency?
- What do we mean by community, collaboration, and collegiality as they pertain to our PLC?
- What commitments are we willing to make to our students this year?
- What commitments are we willing to make to each other as professionals?
- What would our school look like if we decided to assign the most skilled and experienced teachers to the students who need the most help?
- How would our school change if we pursued PLCs?
- What things would be different if we continually asked, "What is best for our students?"

And one final consideration: What are some of the meaningful topics or ideas that can be assigned to a PLC?

+ Create a curriculum map for the entire school.
+ Select a key book, some key articles, or other resources that educators can read and discuss together.
+ Arrange for structured dialogues about consequential education issues.
+ Create interdisciplinary teams in the middle school and the high school to develop curriculum and encourage curriculum coordination.
+ Discuss and create a philosophy of curriculum.
+ Explore the best practices that are already within the school.
+ Create a list of essential questions unique to the school.
+ Define the school's nonnegotiables that flow from the mission of the school.
+ Review and revise the school's mission statement.
+ Review, discuss, and rewrite the school's overall assessment plans.
+ Define the educational outcomes for each course, department, grade level, and school.
+ Embed all individual professional development within the work of the PLC.
+ Mandate specific projects and tasks.

The purpose of PLCs is a simple one: enhancing learning. The wheels to make this car move are the teachers in the school, but the administrators must first turn the key in the ignition. Whether educators can get moving depends on whether they are invested with enough discretion to act, are given the support they need to teach, are involved in continuous learning, and are led by effective leaders. A culture that promotes collaboration, trust, respect, collegiality, and learning for all will generate new learning and add even more competence. "Building capacity among teachers and focusing that capacity on students and their learning is the critical factor. Continuous capacity building and continuous focusing is best done within communities of practice" (Sergiovanni 2000, 140).

Resources on Professional Learning Communities

In addition to the resources cited in the further-reading and reference lists at the end of this book, here are some helpful websites:

All Things PLC: www.allthingsplc.com
This comprehensive website offered by Solution Tree may well have more articles and resources for PLCs than any other single source. Included are (1) an extensive blog and discussion board, (2) research information and hundreds of articles, and (3) hundreds of tools and resources and much more. You could spend weeks investigating this site and still have more to read!

Solution Tree: www.solution-tree.com
This is the website for all the PLC materials available from Solution Tree. It offers materials and events beyond PLCs, but many valuable resources are located on the site.

Note

1. Although *orthopraxy* can be associated with a works-centered theological perspective, as in the case of liberation theology, the term is used here in the same context as James 2:26: "faith without deeds is dead." Biblically, both orthodoxy and orthopraxy must be rooted in grace by faith.

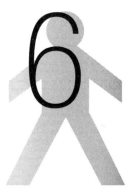

Leadership for Community

The eye cannot say to the hand, "I don't need you!" And the head cannot say to the feet, "I don't need you!" On the contrary, those parts of the body that seem to be weaker are indispensable."
— 1 Corinthians 12:21–22

The proposals suggested in the preceding chapters will not magically occur. Without intentional and persistent systemic changes in the leadership, structure, and relationships within a school, comprehensive induction and professional learning communities (PLCs) will remain, at best, good ideas. The good news is that both induction and PLCs have proved to be effective for educators as well as students. "The research and the practice indicate that schools making the PLC cultural shift will improve the learning in schools and teachers will be more likely to feel a part of the school and want to continue to improve their practices" (Matthews and Crow 2010, 50). The question for Christian schools is whether they have the courage and willingness to change.

Historically, the structures, governance, and pedagogy in schools did not make much room for nourishing community. Frederick Taylor's "scientific management" approach to school administration (addressed in the previous chapter) emphasized efficiency, control, centralization, and standardization; and these emphases led to top-down management, bureaucracy, and a one-size-fits-all approach to schooling (Callahan 1962). Taylorism is still evident in many schools—and it is not conducive to building collegiality, building trust in relationships, and building the community orientation that will enable schools to thrive. Instead, Taylor's approach to schooling and leadership encourages isolation, separation, and mistrust. The leadership structures and school culture either will encourage relationships that are friendly, respectful, and mutually helpful or will continue to promote individualism and competition. And more damaging yet, if schools persist in scientific management and in bureaucratic models of leadership, heads of schools will continue to burn out, change jobs, or find themselves fired by the board when the mythical "superhero" administrator can't get everything done after all. "When leadership turns into management of innumerable imposed initiatives and being evaluated according to unfair and inappropriate forms of accountability, it's not surprising that no one wants to lead anymore" (Hargreaves and Shirley 2009, 96).

This chapter is a synthesis of several leading perspectives for change in educational leadership and an attempt to point Christian schools in a new direction, one in which students and teachers learn more, teachers and administrators share responsibilities and leadership, and biblical norms for relationships and community are more fully realized. The names change, and the models proposed have different titles, but the various authors' concepts are remarkably similar. After summarizing the main contributions to educational leadership theory, the chapter will conclude with some practical applications for Christian school leadership.

Thomas Sergiovanni

Even though the phrases *comprehensive induction* and *professional learning community* don't occur in the dozens of books and articles that Thomas Sergiovanni has written, his generative principles of school leadership paved the way for these innovations. Sergiovanni writes at length about moral leadership, community building, and the critical importance of everyone's faithfully following the mission of the school. "A variety of evidence suggests that schools that function as well-focused communities where unique values are important, where caring for others is the norm, where academic matters count, and where social covenants bring parents, teachers, students, and others into a common commitment get surprisingly good results" (2000, xiii).

Borrowing from the work of the German philosopher Jürgen Habermas, Sergiovanni argues that schools must develop and hold to common purposes, goals, norms, values, and beliefs ("lifeworld") in order to improve the management designs, actions, efficiencies, and policies of administrative leadership ("systemsworld"). He stresses that it's critically important for the lifeworld to serve as the engine driving the school (2000, 5–6). Particularly in Christian schools, the community has the ability to "generate spiritual and social capital," which results in strong educational results in both academics and character development (xi). A major problem comes when the systemsworld begins to "colonize" the lifeworld, a scenario that ultimately erodes the character, culture, and purposes of the school (xiii). The stampede of the standards movement, for example, along with the risks of high-stakes testing, is stripping the unique and individual characteristics from schools and dehumanizing educators and students (viii, 76, 86). To that end, one of the most important roles of the educational leader is to safeguard the lifeworld, to be the chief follower of the mission of the school, and in so doing, to win the battle for purpose and meaning.

Although the protection of the lifeworld is the most important part of leadership, it's crucial to understand that in Sergiovanni's model, the responsibilities and accountabilities for leadership are distributed among all educators. Whether one calls it shared, distributed, participative, or some other type of leadership, the principle is still the same: the wise leader knows that teachers often know more about what needs to be done and how to do it, so he or she shares the leadership with them (2000, 166). In too many schools, the lead administrator is expected to do everything from raising the annual fund to crisis intervention, to discipline, to supervision, to parking lot duty, to even unclogging the toilet!

Think for a moment of a soccer team that is playing a game. As the team moves up and down the field, there is a gracefulness and flow to the action as the ball is advanced toward the net (circumstances change). Both teams are focused on the goal (purpose, mission), and each player fulfills his or her assigned duties (individual educator); but at the same time, the individuals must function as a team (community) in order to achieve success. Certain rules govern the game, and the lines on the field are there for a purpose. But players must be creative, imaginative, coordinated, and observant of ways to help teammates, all the while making split-second decisions on the move. The accountability is very public and immediate—does the team score, will the defense hold, can the goalie make the save? And the team can be victorious only as the members bond together. To be sure, there is a captain on the field, but the leadership and the responsibilities are shared, and the captain knows that he can't be the goalie, the forward, and the defensive back all at once. In Sergiovanni's words, which were quoted in the previous chapter but which bear repeating, the applications to schools are clear: "When levels of collegiality are high, when teachers behave like members of a community of practice, when teachers feel morally obligated to meet their commitments to each other and to the school's purposes, and when teachers are committed to working together to do what is best for students, collective responsibility is high" (2005, 135).

Simon Western

Simon Western (2008) takes a provocative look at the nature of school leadership in *Leadership: A Critical Text*. A quick glance at the Contents page reveals that at least half of the book describes the three main "discourses" of leadership that have dominated over the past one hundred years:

1. *Controller* (scientific management—what Sergiovanni calls the "management engineer" [2007, 7])

2. *Therapist* (human relations—what Sergiovanni labels the "human engineer" [2007, 8])

3. *Messiah* (transformative, servant, and distributed leadership—what Sergiovanni uses two terms to describe, "chief" and "high priest" [2007, 9–10])

Western applies a critical-theory analysis to each, questioning where power and authority reside and what damaging effects (dehumanization, control, manipulation, intimidation, conformity) each discourse can have. He poses some probing questions:

+ Who is sitting at the leadership table?
+ Whose voices are being heard and whose aren't, and why?
+ Whose values are being represented, and on whose behalf?
+ Who is absent from the decision-making process? (2008, 68)

Western then proposes a fourth discourse for leadership, what he labels the "eco-leader," "an emerging leadership discourse which is immersed in leadership practices, values, metaphors and language which resonate with the term ecology" (2008, 183). Eco-leadership stresses connectivity, interdependence, justice, social awareness, and the environment. Eco-leadership advocates a "dispersed leadership" (2), which builds into organizations the ability to be adaptive to fluctuations and constant change (instead of *dispersed leadership*, Sergiovanni may prefer terms like "shared" or "distributed" [2000, 176; 2007, 116]). "The leadership of the future will not be provided simply by individuals but by groups, institutions, communities, and networks" (Western 2008, 186). Western's new leadership model calls for a new ethic, one that takes a critical stance, thinks holistically, understands the nature of authority, and disperses power in the organization. Western is a Quaker, and he acknowledges that the Quaker movement has "informed my understanding of leadership" (4). He uses the Benedictine monastery model, a holistic experience of living and learning in community, as an image for how leadership can function in a school. The monastery, he argues, exercises both a paternal and maternal influence over its members:

> Translated to organizational thinking, the paternal metaphor represents the external, structure, differentiation and reality, while the maternal metaphor represents the internal, unity, oneness, creativity, ideas and play. The paternal metaphor creates a containing structure and space, a place where the maternal metaphor takes over enabling the emotional space for play, creativity and thinking to occur. The paternal metaphor then breaks up this unified bond (mother-infant) to turn their creativity into an outward-facing activity in the "real world." This framework is the basis for all creative and developmental activity and is vital for effective leadership practice. (203)

Too much of an emphasis on the paternal side of things will result in a top-down bureaucratic approach to leadership that has a rigid management structure and little room for adaptation (similar to Sergiovanni's systemsworld, which has a potential to colonize the lifeworld of leadership). By contrast, a heavy emphasis on the maternal side can open the door to exclusivity, to creating an inward-focused school with cultlike tendencies that disparages others (Western 2008, 204).

Western argues that leadership is not a set of skills, a learned profession, or a formula to follow, but rather a complex and holistic process of formation within school systems that is constantly changing. Leadership, he argues, emerges in the midst of community as groups of individuals take on responsibility for particular tasks, so successful organizations creatively design the structures that allow for leadership to surface as learning takes place. "Management is closely associated with efficiency and control, there is nothing wrong with this, it is very important. Leadership is associated with moving forward, taking authority, creating change through influencing.... The 'Holy Grail' of leadership is to be found when we stop searching for it, and see that it is all around us, in the processes, behaviours, and the social systems in which we work on a daily basis" (2008, 39–40). This can be disconcerting for many heads of schools in that it feels like letting go of too much authority and control, but "paradoxically, this discourse finds that the real vulnerability of leadership lies in control, hierarchy and omnipotence. The real strength of leadership lies in devolved power, dispersing leadership and having the confidence of not-knowing, of being able to follow emergent patterns, rather than fixed plans" (197).

For leaders of Christian schools, who frequently have too daunting a list of assignments while other educators and leaders in the building feel stymied by their lack of leadership, Western's eco-leadership model offers some new paths for the development of PLCs: "Leadership ... steps back from the grandiosity and the hubris of the Messiah discourse, which aims at the transformation of organizations and followers.... Leadership exists all around us, but so much of it presently goes unnoticed and is uncherished, at the expense of organizational success and social well-being. It takes time, the right conditions and the right support to nurture the 'leader within.' The leader within oneself, and the leadership within the organization, both need nurturing and sustaining" (2008, 208).

Stephanie Pace Marshall

Stephanie Pace Marshall argues that schools need a whole new language, a whole new story, or a whole new structure—one that is rooted in connectedness and community. "Mentally, emotionally, and spiritually out of breath, many children are hyperventilating from frenzied trivial pursuit and excessive activity.... Nothing seems connected. Patterns are unclear; only things and events matter" (2006, 13). What we have lost in schooling, she contends, is a sense of interdependence, imagination, and integration (176).

Using the same approach as others, Marshall passionately argues for an organic orientation toward learning. "Although learning is the creative process of life, our current learning story conceives it as a mechanistic, prescribed, and easily measured commodity that can be incrementally and uniformly delivered to our children. This narrative could not be more wrong" (2006, 38).

"The most significant work of our time will be integrative" (2006, 46), declares Marshall, and then she describes six characteristics of this new landscape for generative learning (viii):

1. *Integrity*—honesty about what intelligence really is
2. *Vibrancy*—learning environments growing and developing on the "fuel" of information
3. *Interdependence*—key relationships of various kinds
4. *Coherence*—connection of learning with the big questions in life
5. *Sustainability*—students seeing the whole, things making sense to them
6. *Stability*—encouragement of "deep learning" that is interactive, imaginative, and often messy

And she is optimistic that change can occur: "Our cultural mind is slowly shifting from fragmentation and reductionism, expressed in excessive competition, unbridled acquisition, winning, short-term thinking, and isolated self-interest, to integration and interdependence—collaboration, shared purpose, and global sustainability" (179).

Marshall concludes her book with an extended call for the emergence of "elder leaders" (similar in many ways to Western's eco-leader), leaders who can help construct this new narrative for schooling. This is not the old "command and control" leadership but a leadership that is rooted in meaning, deep learning, wholeness, belonging, patterns, and structures (2006, 191–96). "Our children want to learn and engage in lives of meaning, purpose, connection, and contribution while they are still young.... Our children don't want to be passive observers in their own learning. They want to be in the center with us" (189).

Similar to Western's Benedictine monk metaphor of the paternal and maternal eco-leader, the leader that Marshall envisions is a radically different type of school leader: "Elders are called to teach and cocreate a covenant of meaning and belonging with the young; nurture and prepare them through life-affirming stories and initiations; infuse their present with the wisdom of the past; and affirm their future possibilities. Elders hold the context (story), consciousness (meaning), and soul (wisdom) of a culture" (2006, 193).

Andy Hargreaves and Dennis Shirley

So, how can schools pull off such dramatic change in leadership, professionalism, community orientation, and accountability? At this point the temptation may be to think that the problems are too pressing, the new proposals too daunting, and the path to change too-often lined with many rocks and obstacles. But then comes *The Fourth Way: The Inspiring Future for Educational Change* by Andy Hargreaves and Dennis Shirley (2009), and suddenly a way out of the thicket becomes visible—a reasonable road to significant educational change and improvement appears.

Hargreaves and Shirley (2009) begin their book by summarizing the first three "ways" that have appeared in education since World War II:

1. The first wave of educational change (1940s–1970s) was marked by intense but inconsistent innovation (3). Educators experienced a great deal of freedom and autonomy, but they lacked a corresponding development of leadership that ensured consistency. It was a creative and sometimes rebellious period (remember the "new math" of the 1960s and the reading strategies that didn't include phonics?). But as time went on, the desire for coherence, standardization, and better leadership ushered in a new wave of common curriculum and standardization.

2. The second wave (1980s–1990s) was characterized by standardization, bureaucracy, and uniformity, but at the loss of the freedom, creativity, and trust of the first wave (12). In the center of this wave, in 1980, the U.S. Department of Education was created during President Carter's term of office. As centralization grew, however, test scores plateaued, teacher motivation and morale declined, and teacher retention began to decrease. Thus, the publication in 1983 of the national report *A Nation at Risk: The Imperative for Educational Reform* led to numerous educational reform movements.

3. The third wave (1990s–the first decade of the twenty-first century) sought to bring these two waves together in order to balance professional autonomy with accountability (12). Inspired by change authorities like Michael Fullan (2001, 2008), this third wave started off well, but it was "distracted" into what Hargreaves and Shirley call the "New Orthodoxy": top-down mandates about testing, a "technocratic obsession with data," and an overindulgence in looking for "quick-fix strategies" that could then be documented through "Adequate Yearly Progress" results (2009, xi, 40). "In the New Orthodoxy, schools don't just react to testing, targets, and Adequate Yearly Progress. Instead, they anticipate and prepare for them—with a vengeance" (40). The No Child Left Behind (NCLB) legislation of 2001 is the best example of how the third wave fell into this new orthodoxy. Diane Ravitch, the education professor who served under both President Bush and President Clinton, originally supported NCLB but recently wrote, "I became disillusioned with the strategies that once seemed so promising. I no longer believe that either approach [accountability or school choice] will produce the quantum improvement in American education that we all hope for" (2010).

Unlike the "Third Way" (or the "third wave" above), the "Fourth Way," advocated by Hargreaves and Shirley, is one in which teachers and schools are liberated to pursue professionalism and learning, free from the grip of government controls and high-stakes testing. Although their book has the public education system in view, their vision of change and accountability is applicable for Christian education as well. In reality, many of their fourth-way principles sound similar to the PLCs described in the previous chapter of this book: "This is the essence of the idea of professional learning communities, where leaders pull responsible, qualified, and highly capable teachers together in pursuit of improvement within a culture that celebrates persistent questioning and celebration of the art and craft of teaching" (2009, 87).

Hargreaves and Shirley (2009) describe four catalysts that will make these fourth-way changes happen:
1. *Sustaining and distributing leadership:* "Distributed leadership creates pools among classroom teachers from which future higher-level leaders come. It entails developing leadership early among many, and not just among the chosen few who show obvious potential" (96).

2. *Creating "networks" (what others call PLCs), both within and outside schools, that enable educators to learn from one another:* "The point of networks is to spread innovation, stimulate learning, increase professional motivation, and reduce inequities" (101).

3. *Emphasizing responsibility before accountability:* "The Fourth Way treats accountability as the conscience or superego of the system that checks it, not as the ego or id that drives it" (103).

4. *Creating systems for and allowing the freedom for differentiation and diversity to counter the drive toward a restrictive standardization of curriculum* (104)

This fourth-way vision for educational change and accountability advocates high standards and expectations, liberates teachers, and encourages students to become vigorous and active partners in learning. As the authors describe it toward the end of their book,

> In the Fourth Way, there will be standards, including public, human, business, and ethical ones, but there will no longer be educational standardization. There will also be targets, and these will be even bolder because dedicated professionals will identify them together. There will be hard work and persistence, but not pointless drudgery. There will be greater support for the education profession, but not unconditionally. Accountability will be our conscience, not our Grand Inquisitor. And our children will be the deposits of learning, generosity, and humanity through which we invest in the future. (111)

Implications for Leadership

A school is a school. That may sound like an odd statement, but Christian educators sometimes need to be reminded of that fact. Parents invest the tuition, and students come through the doors expecting to learn; and it's the task of the Christian school to be a school, to provide a comprehensive, challenging, and God-honoring education. Learning is the primary focus of a school, and that's a good place to start.

But what makes a good school? The following are some common descriptions and characteristics that should be considered by Christian schools:

+ A common sense of purpose
+ Teachers and students who learn together
+ Celebration of accomplishments
+ Development of students' critical-thinking and problem-solving skills

+ Curiosity and creativity regularly encouraged by the curriculum
+ Development of interpersonal skills
+ Respect for and celebration of differences
+ Rich and challenging academics
+ Active cocurricular programs
+ Effective, regular, and comprehensive assessment programs
+ Teachers who work together toward success for all students
+ An evident variety of teaching and learning strategies
+ A safe, orderly, and welcoming environment
+ Open and friendly collaboration and collegiality
+ A staff of educators who are regarded as professionals and are encouraged to grow
+ Shared leadership in decision making

All of these objectives and more can be pursued within PLCs under the models of leadership described in this chapter. As the research demonstrates, "When teachers have structured opportunities to explore the nitty-gritty challenges of their practice through thoughtful exchanges with colleagues and in relation to relevant research, they rediscover the passion for learning and their own personal and professional growth that brought them into teaching in the first place" (Hargreaves and Shirley 2009, 93).

So what framework will facilitate these consequential conversations, this sort of enthusiasm, this level of growth and learning for both faculty and students?

Community

We must use community as our theory of practice. Schools as communities must be characterized by loyalty, commitment, sacrifice, and values; they must be environments in which sacrificing one's own self-interest for the sake of the common good is the norm. In a community, members share fellowship, personal relationships, and commitments with one another. The unique and distinctive practices of the school community are part of what binds the members together and leads to collegial practice. The community must ask itself these questions: "What are we about? What is distinctive about our school? What are we responsible for? To whom are we responsible? How do we cause our beliefs to be embodied in our actions? What is our definition and practice of education?" All of these questions imply promises, obligations, responsibilities, and accountability.

Connections

Connections are everything. Typical leadership programs emphasize control and authority, but this emphasis militates against community. What makes for a quality Christian school is the aggregate of the teachers and administrators working and striving together, and the "together" part happens only within relationships. Shared practice as opposed to individual practice must become the expectation, because we know that the sum of the whole is always superior to the individual parts. The students must also be connected to the teachers, and everyone must be connected to the vision and mission of the school.

Vision

The school vision must be made useful. A critical first step for leadership is to ensure that the mission and vision statements of the school are clearly expressed and understood, and that these statements are the nexus for every curricular and cocurricular decision. The mission statement tells what the school is about while the vision statement pictures where the school is going. These statements must guide the following questions: What are the responsibilities of each group? What promises do the constituent groups (faculty, administration, staff, students, parents, board) make to one another? How do we agree to make decisions in ways that don't cut off certain groups? Are we willing to eliminate a program or an activity when it is clear that it doesn't fit the mission of the school? The answers need to be spelled out and articulated for all school groups, but the process alone will create a powerful source of authority.

Ideas

Lead with ideas. This is a key concept in Sergiovanni's view of school leadership. Leadership by position, personality, or charisma is not the most powerful source of authority in his view. Instead he advocates a "followership" in which everyone follows the ideas and ideals of the school, and everything and everyone must be in service to those beliefs and ideas. One of the key functions of leadership is to hold the school to the mission and the vision, and to express outrage when things get off kilter (2000, 167; 1992, 130). If the school decides to pursue comprehensive induction and PLCs, then the cooperation and planning for those changes will need to be rooted in the ideas and the mission.

Community, connections, vision, ideas—it may be tempting to view these words as too ideal or too philosophical for the typical Christian school, but that very temptation may be an indication that the school leader and the school need the ideas presented in this book more than they know. This framework does not represent the frills and adornments for only a few elite schools. Rather, its components must serve as the building blocks for all Christian schools serious about leading students into an authentic relationship with Jesus Christ and about equipping them for passionate engagement in His kingdom.

A Personal Example

In the summer of 2010, I participated for the fourth time in the five-hundred-mile *Register's* Annual Great Bicycle Ride Across Iowa (RAGBRAI). Nearly twenty thousand people gathered on the west side of the state in late July, dipped their back tire in the Missouri River, then rode east for seven days to dip their front tire in the Mississippi River. RAGBRAI is a wonderful tradition, a great week of exercise and fellowship, and a real slice of Americana. But it's also a great example of community-in-action since many riders come with family and friends and ride as a group. Those relationships are visible every day as riders help, encourage, and exhort one another. I've seen some people pedaling up a steep hill while pushing with one hand on their partner's lower back to help the partner make it up the hill. I've seen riders who have stopped to help others who have fallen or gotten hurt or experienced mechanical problems. This past summer I had to stop and fix a flat tire, and I must have been asked several dozen times in ten minutes whether I needed any help. Riders are constantly yelling "Car up!" (as a vehicle approaches) or "Rumbles!" (to warn of rumble strips[1] ahead) or "On your left!" (for a safe passing lane)—all to communicate safety and other important information to other riders. I've seen people sharing, giving food and drinks away, and doing other kind and charitable things that help make the experience good, safe, and rewarding for the participants. There is a palpable sense of community on RAGBRAI, a sense of "we are all in this together and we need each other in order to succeed."

A week of RAGBRAI parallels a school setting in several ways. Teachers, administrators, students, parents, and board members could all learn to pull in the same direction to make Christian schooling a fulfilling and rich experience for everyone concerned. Schools could work together to end the isolation, competition, infighting, and mistrust and to replace these negative realities with true community and with relationships built on honesty, support, and trust.

The key to this school unity, of course, is found in the grace and love of Jesus Christ. The more we understand, believe, and live in the grace of God toward us as individuals—that my sins are far worse than I want to imagine, but that Christ's forgiveness is real and complete and more than a match for my sin—the more we will realize our utter dependence on the mercy of Jesus for ourselves *and* for those with whom we work. The more our love for Jesus grows, the more we will find ourselves loving others as brothers and sisters in Jesus—not viewing them as sinners and failures, but learning to view them as they are in Christ—coheirs clothed with the perfect righteousness of Jesus (Romans 4:24, 8:17). This is the community and vision that will provide the fuel for a school to move forward; so dip your rear tire and start pedaling.

Note

1. Rumble strips are portions of a paved road that have been altered to cause vibration and sound when vehicles drive over them.

Conclusion

The command to teach our covenant children is as old as Deuteronomy 6:4–9, the Jewish confession of faith known as the Shema, in which God's people are instructed to "impress" the law of God on their children at all times and in all places so that "they would put their trust in God" (as Psalm 78:7 envisions). As the Old Testament time line progressed, the synagogue developed (during the period of exile) for, among other things, educational purposes. In the New Testament, Paul, like Jesus, demonstrates a high regard for children and their education, exhorting fathers to "bring them up in the training and instruction of the Lord" (Ephesians 6:4). The biblical emphasis on families, children, and a godly upbringing is significant.

The Heritage of Christian Schooling
We find a similar heritage in the history of the Christian Church through the writings and influences of patriarchs and other authors.

Augustine
Saint Augustine taught that all truth is God's truth, and in book 1 of *Confessions*, he famously wrote, "Thou madest us for Thyself, and our heart is restless, until it repose in Thee" (1996, 1.1[1]). All education, therefore, was religious by definition.

Erasmus of Rotterdam

Desiderius Erasmus of Rotterdam was even more direct: "All studies, philosophy, rhetoric are followed for this one object, that we may know Christ and honor him. This is the end of all learning and eloquence" (Lockerbie 1986, 201).

From the Protestant Reformation and forward, we hear the following:

Martin Luther

Martin Luther didn't mince any words either: "For we certainly want to provide not only for our children's bellies, but for their souls as well.... I would advise no one to send his child where the Holy Scriptures are not supreme" (Tappert 1967, 41, 343).

John Calvin

John Calvin established an academy in Geneva, Switzerland, because like other reformers, he understood that the Reformation needed an educated laity and that education must be rooted in the Bible. The school opened in 1559, providing free tuition to children of poor parents. It became a model for other schools throughout Europe and North America. The ultimate educational objective of the Genevan Academy was the inculcation of the knowledge of God and His works for the purpose of God's glory and Christian service to humankind. Calvin wrote, "The Word of God indeed is the foundation of all learning, but the liberal arts are aids to the full knowledge of the Word and not to be despised" (Monroe 1919, 491).

Richard Baxter

The English Puritan preacher Richard Baxter valued education: "Education is God's ordinary way for the conveyance of his grace, and ought no more to be set in opposition to the Spirit than the preaching of the Word" (Ryken 1986, 159).

Harvard College

A pamphlet titled *New England's First Fruits* (Weld and Peter 1643) lists the founding "Rules and Precepts" of Harvard College, a school begun by theologians from the Reformation. The second rule states, "Let every Student be plainly instructed, and earnestly pressed to consider well, the maine end of his life and studies is, *to know God and Jesus Christ which is eternall life,* Joh[n] 17.3, and therefore to lay *Christ* in the bottome, as the only foundation of all sound knowledge and Learning" (Cubberley 1920, 292).

J. Gresham Machen

In the twentieth century, J. Gresham Machen writes, "A truly Christian education is possible only when Christian conviction underlies not a part, but all, of the curriculum of the school. True learning and true piety go hand in hand, and Christianity embraces the whole of life—those are great central convictions that underlie the Christian school" (1987, 81).

Why This Overview?

What's the point of this brief biblical and historical overview? Simply this: Christian schooling enjoys a glorious and rich heritage on which both the present demands and opportunities and the future dreams and aspirations can be built. This book addresses one of the crucial needs for Christian schools today, that is, enhancing and increasing the professional rigor of all teachers while creating an environment for deep learning for all. It is encouraging and hopeful to remember that our work today is part of a fabric that has been woven over the centuries, even though we are usually able to see only a small part of a much larger picture.

Recently I was on an early morning flight from Saint Louis to Chicago, and there was a low level of clouds below the plane but a beautifully clear, cobalt-blue sky above. About halfway to Chicago, the light in the eastern sky became brighter and brighter as the sun was about to appear on the horizon. I actually moved from one side of the plane to the other just so I could watch, but since it was a short flight, the plane began to descend into Chicago rather quickly. Once or twice the smallest sliver of the sun would appear but then quickly disappear again below the horizon. Soon the plane dropped below the cloud cover, and my hopes of witnessing the sun rise from the air vanished. I got only a brief glimpse.

When I think of Christian schooling that is rooted in God's grace, designed with real and vital community as a priority, structured in ways that encourage and support educators to grow and lead professionally, and always centered on learning, I think it must be a glimpse of what heaven will be like. It's a foretaste of glory divine.

Note

1. Chapter 1, page 1.

Further Reading

Introduction

Alliance for Excellent Education. 2004. *Tapping the potential: Retaining and developing high-quality new teachers.* Washington, DC: Alliance for Excellent Education.

Chapter 3

Bartell, Carol A. 2004. *Cultivating high-quality teaching through induction and mentoring.* Thousand Oaks, CA: Corwin Press.

Brock, Barbara L., and Marilyn L. Grady. 2005. *Developing a teacher induction plan: A guide for school leaders.* Thousand Oaks, CA: Corwin Press.

Hare, Debra, and James L. Heep. 2001. *Effective teacher recruitment and retention strategies in the Midwest: Who is making use of them?* Naperville, IL: North Central Regional Education Laboratory.

Ingersoll, Richard M. 2001. Teacher turnover and teacher shortages: An organizational analysis. *American Educational Research Journal* 38, no. 3 (September): 499–534.

———. 2003. *Is there really a teacher shortage?* Center for the Study of Teaching and Policy. Seattle, WA: Univ. of Washington.

Ingersoll, Richard M., and Thomas M. Smith. 2003. The wrong solution to the teacher shortage. *Educational Leadership* 60, no. 8 (May): 30–33.

Millinger, Cynthia Simon. 2004. Helping new teachers cope. *Educational Leadership* 61, no. 8 (May): 66–69.

Morgan, Jill, and Betty Ashbaker. 2000. Supporting new teachers: Practical suggestions for experienced staff. *Rural Educator* 22, no. 1 (Fall): 35–37.

Patterson, Mary. 2005. Hazed! *Educational Leadership* 62, no. 8 (May): 20–23.

Pierce, Cecilia, and Janice Patterson. 2006. A new vision: A role for teacher educators in teacher induction. Paper presented at the annual meeting of the American Association of Colleges for Teacher Education, San Diego, January 30.

Portner, Hal, ed. 2005. *Teacher mentoring and induction: The state of the art and beyond.* Thousand Oaks, CA: Corwin Press.

Villani, Susan. 2005. *Mentoring and induction programs that support new principals.* Thousand Oaks, CA: Corwin Press.

Wong, Harry K., Ted Britton, and Tom Ganser. 2005. What the world can teach us about new teacher induction. *Phi Delta Kappan* 86, no. 5 (January): 379–84.

Wong, Harry K., and Rosemary Wong. 2010. Significant research and readings on comprehensive induction. http://www.newteacher.com/pdf/Significant_Research_on_Induction.pdf (accessed April 6, 2011).

Chapter 5

DuFour, Richard, and Robert Eaker. 1998. *Professional learning communities at work: Best practices for enhancing student achievement.* Alexandria, VA: Solution Tree.

Marshall, Stephanie Pace. 2006. *The power to transform: Leadership that brings learning and schooling to life.* San Francisco: Jossey-Bass.

Mitchell, Carrie Lynn. 2007. The use of two professional learning community practices in elementary classrooms and the English language arts achievement of California's most at-risk student subgroups in a Southern California school district. Dissertation, Pepperdine Univ., March.

Mouw, Richard J. 2004. *Calvinism in the Las Vegas airport: Making connections in today's world.* Grand Rapids, MI: Zondervan.

Chapter 6

Ravitch, Diane. 2010. *The death and life of the great American school system: How testing and choice are undermining education.* New York: Basic Books.

References

Alliance for Excellent Education. 2004. *Tapping the potential: Retaining and developing high-quality new teachers*. Washington, DC: Alliance for Excellent Education.

Augustine. 1996. *Confessions*. Trans. Edward Bouverie Pusey. New York: Book-of-the-Month Club.

Baker College Effective Teaching and Learning Department. 2004. Teaching across generations. http://www.mcc.edu/pdf/pdo/teaching_across_gen.pdf.

Barth, Roland S. 2002. The culture builder. *Educational Leadership* 59, no. 8 (May): 6–11.

_____. 2006. Improving relationships within the schoolhouse. *Educational Leadership* 63, no. 6 (March): 8–13.

Bassett, Patrick F. 2003. Great teachers: Is "high quality" the same as "highly qualified"? *Education Week* 22, no. 24 (February 26): 26–28.

Black, Susan. 2004. Helping teachers helps keep them around. *Education Digest* 70, no. 4 (December): 46–51.

Bonhoeffer, Dietrich. 1954. *Life together*. Trans. John W. Doberstein. New York: HarperCollins.

Bowers, C. A. 1987. *Elements of a post-liberal theory of education*. New York: Teachers College Press. Cited in Stronks and Blomberg 1993, 172.

Brookfield, S. 2003. Putting the critical back in critical pedagogy: A commentary on the path of dissent. *Journal of Transformative Education* 1:141–49. Quoted in Servage 2008, 66.

Brophy, J., and T. Good. 2002. *Looking in classrooms*. 9th ed. Boston: Allyn and Bacon. Cited in DuFour 2007b.

Callahan, Raymond E. 1962. *Education and the cult of efficiency: A study of the social forces that have shaped the administration of the public schools*. Univ. of Chicago Press.

Carver, Cynthia L., and Daniel S. Katz. 2004. Teaching at the boundary of acceptable practice: What is a new teacher mentor to do? *Journal of Teacher Education* 55, no. 5 (November–December): 449–62.

Cochran-Smith, Marilyn. 2004. Stayers, leavers, lovers, and dreamers: Insights about teacher retention. *Journal of Teacher Education* 55, no. 5 (November–December): 387–92.

Cohen, M. D. 1991. Individual learning and organizational routine: Emerging connections. *Organizational Science* 2, no. 1:135–39. Cited in Louis 2006, 481.

Collins, Jim. 2001. *Good to great: Why some companies make the leap … and others don't.* New York: HarperBusiness.

Csikszentmihalyi, Mihaly. 1997. *Finding flow: The psychology of engagement with everyday life.* MasterMinds series. New York: Basic Books.

Cuban, Larry. 1992. Managing dilemmas while building professional communities. *Educational Researcher* 21, no. 1 (January–February): 4–11. Cited in Louis 2006, 478.

Cubberley, Ellwood P. 1920. *Readings in the history of education: A collection of sources and readings to illustrate the development of educational practice, theory, and organization.* Cambridge, MA: Riverside Press.

Danielson, Charlotte, and Thomas McGreal. 2000. *Teacher evaluation to enhance professional practice.* Alexandria, VA: Association for Supervision and Curriculum Development and Educational Testing Service. Cited in Black 2004.

Darling-Hammond, Linda. 2000. Teacher quality and student achievement: A review of state policy evidence. *Educational Policy Analysis Archives* 8, no. 1. Cited in Darling-Hammond and Youngs 2002, 16. http://epaa.asu.edu/epaa/v8n1.

Darling-Hammond, Linda, and Peter Youngs. 2002. Defining "highly qualified teachers": What does "scientifically-based research" actually tell us? *Educational Researcher* 31, no 9 (December): 13–25.

Doerger, Daniel W. 2003. The importance of beginning teacher induction in your school. *International Electronic Journal for Leadership in Learning* 7. http://www.ucalgary.ca/iejll/+Daniel+W.+Doerger.

Drexler, James L., ed. 2007. *Schools as communities: Educational leadership, relationships, and the eternal value of Christian schooling.* Colorado Springs, CO: Purposeful Design Publications.

DuFour, Richard. 2007a. In praise of top-down leadership: What drives your school improvement efforts—evidence of best practice or the pursuit of universal buy-in? *School Administrator* 64, no. 10.

————. 2007b. Professional learning communities: A bandwagon, an idea worth considering, or our best hope for high levels of learning? *Middle School Journal* 39, no. 1 (September): 4–8.

Eaker, Robert, and Janel Keating. 2008. A shift in school culture: Collective commitments focus on change that benefits student learning. *Journal of Staff Development* 29, no. 3 (Summer): 14–17.

Elmore, Richard F. 2004. *School reform from the inside out: Policy, practice, and performance.* Cambridge, MA: Harvard Education Press. Cited in DuFour 2007a and Fullan 2008, 86.

Feiman-Nemser, Sharon. 2000. Introd. to *New teacher induction: Programs, policies and practice.* Unpublished report. National Partnership for Excellence and Accountability in Education. Cited in Carver and Katz 2004, 450.

————. 2003. What new teachers need to learn. *Educational Leadership* 60, no. 8 (May): 25–29.

Ferguson, Ronald F. 1998. Teachers' perceptions and expectations and the black-white test score gap. In *The black-white test score gap*, ed. Christopher Jencks and Meredith Phillips, 273–317. Washington, DC: Brookings Institution Press.

Fullan, Michael. 2001. *Leading in a culture of change: Being effective in complex times.* San Francisco: Jossey-Bass.

————. 2006. Leading professional learning. *School Administrator* 63, no. 10 (November): 10.

————. 2008. *The six secrets of change: What the best leaders do to help their organizations survive and thrive.* San Francisco: Jossey-Bass.

Gilbert, Linda. 2005. What helps beginning teachers? *Educational Leadership* 62, no. 8 (May): 36–39.

Gitomer, Drew H. 2007. *Teacher quality in a changing policy landscape: Improvements in the teacher pool.* Princeton, NJ: Educational Testing Service.

Gladwell, Malcolm. 2008. Most likely to succeed: How do we hire when we can't tell who's right for the job? *New Yorker* 84, no. 41 (December 15): 36.

Grenz, Stanley L. 2000. *Renewing the center: Evangelical theology in a post-theological era.* Grand Rapids, MI: BridgePoint Books. Quoted in Drexler 2007, xiv.

Groome, Thomas. 1980. *Christian religious education: Sharing our story and vision.* San Francisco: Harper and Row. Cited in Van Dyk 2001, 48.

Grossman, Pamela, Sam Wineburg, and Stephen Woolworth. 2001. Toward a theory of teacher community. *Teachers College Record* 103, no. 6:942–1,012.

Halford, Joan Montgomery. 1998. Easing the way for new teachers. *Educational Leadership* 55, no. 5 (February): 33–36.

Hargreaves, Andy, and Dennis Shirley. 2009. *The fourth way: The inspiring future for educational change.* Thousand Oaks, CA: Corwin.

Hekman, Bruce. 2007. Schools as communities of grace: Flourishing as living water and living stones. In Drexler 2007, 3–22.

Hord, Shirley M. 1997. Professional learning communities: Communities of continuous inquiry and improvement. http://www.sedl.org/pubs/change34/welcome.html.

———. 2008. Evolution of the professional learning community: Revolutionary concept is based on intentional collegial learning. *Journal of Staff Development* 29, no. 3 (Summer): 10–13.

Horn, Patty J., Hillary A. Sterling, Heidi C. Blair, and Kristin Metler-Armijo. 2006. Induction strategies for future teachers. Paper presented at the American Association of Colleges for Teacher Education, San Diego, January.

Huling-Austin, Leslie. 1990. Teacher induction programs and internships. In *Handbook of research on teacher education*, ed. W. R. Houston, R. Howsam, and J. Sikula, 535–48. New York: Macmillan. Quoted in Doerger 2003.

Ingersoll, Richard M. 2002. The teacher shortage: A case of wrong diagnosis and wrong prescription. *NASSP Bulletin* 86, no. 631:16–31. Cited in Millinger 2004, 66.

————. 2003. *Is there really a teacher shortage?* Center for the Study of Teaching and Policy. Seattle, WA: Univ. of Washington.

Ingersoll, Richard M., and Jeffrey M. Kralik. 2004. *The impact of mentoring on teacher retention: What the research says.* Denver, CO: Education Commission of the States.

Ingersoll, Richard M., and Thomas M. Smith. 2003. The wrong solution to the teacher shortage. *Educational Leadership* 60, no. 8 (May): 30–33.

Johnson, Shelly J. 2004. Feeding, not eating, our young: Creating effective induction programs for first-year teachers. Unpublished manuscript, Covenant College, Lookout Mountain, GA.

Johnson, Susan Moore, and Susan M. Kardos. 2005. Bridging the generation gap. *Educational Leadership* 62, no. 8 (May): 8–14.

Keenan, Derek. 2000–2001. Cultivating belonging in the school staff. *Christian School Education* 4, no. 5:16–18.

Kelley, Linda Molner. 2004. Why induction matters. *Journal of Teacher Education* 55, no. 5 (November–December): 438–48.

Kersten, Denise. 2006. Watch over me: Teacher-induction programs seem to work best when mentors are given enough time and resources to do their jobs well. *Teacher Magazine,* January–February, 9–10.

Kleine-Kracht, P. A. 1993. The principal in a community of learning. *Journal of School Leadership* 3, no. 4:391–99.

Knowles, Malcolm S. 1980. *The modern practice of adult education: From pedagogy to andragogy.* Englewood Cliffs, NJ: Cambridge Adult Education.

Koops, Barry. 2009. The quarterback problem. Leadership Insights blog. http://csionline.org/leadershipinsights/?p=124 (posted January 7).

Kounin, Jacob. 1970. *Discipline and group management in classrooms.* New York: Holt, Rinehart and Winston.

Lezotte, L. 1997. *Learning for all.* Okemos, MI: Effective Schools Products. Cited in DuFour 2007b.

Lieberman, Ann, and Lynne Miller, eds. 2008. *Teachers in professional communities: Improving teaching and learning.* Series on School Reform. New York: Teachers College Press.

Little, J. W. 1990. The persistence of privacy: Autonomy and initiative in teachers' professional relations. *Teachers College Record* 91:509–36. Cited in DuFour 2007b.

Little, J. W., and J. S. Horn. 2007. "Normalizing" problems of practice: Converting routine conversation into a resource for learning in professional communities. In *Professional learning communities: Divergence, depth, and dilemmas,* ed. L. Stoll and K. S. Louis, 79–92. Maidenhead, England: Open Univ. Press. Quoted in Lieberman and Miller 2008, 20.

Lockerbie, D. Bruce. 1986. Thinking like a Christian, part 3: A call for Christian humanism. Cited in *Bibliotheca Sacra* 143 (July): 195–204.

Louis, Karen Seashore. 2006. Changing the culture of schools: Professional community, organizational learning, and trust. *Journal of School Leadership* 16, no. 4 (September): 477–89.

Machen, J. Gresham. 1987. *Education, Christianity, and the state.* Jefferson, MD: Trinity Foundation.

Makkonen, Reino. 2004. Taking care of novice teachers. *Harvard Education Letter* 20, no. 3 (May–June).

Many, Tom, and Dennis King. 2008. Districts speak with one voice: Clarity and coherence come from professional learning communities. *Journal of Staff Development* 29, no. 3 (Summer): 28–30.

Marshall, Stephanie Pace. 2006. *The power to transform: Leadership that brings learning and schooling to life.* San Francisco: Jossey-Bass.

Marzano, R. 2003. *What works in schools: Translating research into action.* Alexandria, VA: Association for Supervision and Curriculum Development. Cited in DuFour 2007b.

Matthews, L. Joseph, and Gary M. Crow. 2010. *The principalship: New roles in a professional learning community.* Boston, MA: Allyn and Bacon.

McCann, Thomas M., Larry R. Johannessen, and Bernard Ricca. 2005. Responding to new teachers' concerns. *Educational Leadership* 62, no. 8 (May): 30–34.

McLaughlin, Milbrey Wallin. 1992. How district communities do and do not foster teacher pride. *Educational Leadership* 50, no. 1 (September): 33–35. Cited in Louis 2006, 478.

Michigan Education Association. 2000. *Educational Testing Service presents a mentoring institute.* Brochure. East Lansing, MI: Michigan Education Association. Cited in Feiman-Nemser 2003, 25.

Millinger, Cynthia Simon. 2004. Helping new teachers cope. *Educational Leadership* 61, no. 8 (May): 66–69.

Mitchell, Coral, and Larry Sackney. 2006. Building schools, building people: The school principal's role in leading a learning community. *Journal of School Leadership* 16, no. 5 (September): 627–40.

Moir, Ellen. 2000. The stages of a teacher's first year. Appendix to *Help me! I'm New! Inducting and mentoring teachers new to your Christian school,* 18–22. Ancaster, ON, Canada: Ontario Alliance of Christian Schools.

Moller, Gayle. 2006. Teacher leadership emerges within professional learning communities. *Journal of School Leadership* 16, no. 5 (September): 520–33.

Monroe, Paul. 1919. *A cyclopedia of education.* Vol. 1. New York: Macmillan.

Mouw, Richard J. 2004. *Calvinism in the Las Vegas airport: Making connections in today's world.* Grand Rapids, MI: Zondervan. Quoted in Drexler 2007, xiv.

Nabors, A. Randy. 2009. We need to get our 'ortho' straight. Sermon presented at New City Fellowship, Chattanooga, TN, June 14.

Oppewal, Donald. 1985. Biblical knowing and teaching. Monograph, Calvin College. http://www.calvin.edu/academic/education/news/publications/monoweb/teaching.pdf.

Ostrander, Rick. 2009. *Why college matters to God: Academic faithfulness and Christian higher education.* Abilene, TX: Abilene Christian Univ. Press.

Palmer, Parker. 1998. *The courage to teach: Exploring the inner landscape of a teacher's life.* 1st ed. San Francisco: Jossey-Bass.

Ravitch, Diane. 2010. Why I changed my mind about school reform. *Wall Street Journal,* March 10. http://online.wsj.com/article/SB100014240527 48704869304575109443305343962.html.

Rebore, Ronald W., and Angela L. E. Walmsley. 2010. *Recruiting and retaining Generation Y teachers.* Thousand Oaks, CA: Corwin Press.

Reeves, D. 2006. *The learning leader: How to focus school improvement for better results.* Alexandria, VA: Association for Supervision and Curriculum Development. Cited in DuFour 2007b.

Renard, Lisa. 2003. Setting new teachers up for failure ... or success. *Educational Leadership* 60, no. 8 (May): 62–64.

Rice, J. K. 2003. *Teacher quality: Understanding the effectiveness of teacher attributes.* Washington, DC: Economic Policy Institute.

Ripley, Amanda. 2010. What makes a great teacher? *Atlantic* 305, no. 1 (January–February): 58–66.

Roy, Patricia, and Shirley M. Hord. 2006. It's everywhere, but what is it? Professional learning communities. *Journal of School Leadership* 16, no. 5 (September): 490–501.

Ryken, Leland. 1986. *Worldly saints: The Puritans as they were.* Grand Rapids, MI: Zondervan.

Schön, Donald A. 1983. *The reflective practitioner. How professionals think in action.* New York: Basic Books. Quoted in Lieberman and Miller 2008, 21.

———— 1987. *Educating the reflective practitioner: Toward a new design for teaching and learning in the professions.* Higher Education Series. San Francisco: Jossey-Bass.

Senge, Peter, Nelda Cambron-McCabe, Timothy Lucas, Bryan Smith, Janis Dutton, and Art Kleiner. 2000. *Schools that learn: A fifth discipline fieldbook for educators, parents, and everyone who cares about education.* New York: Doubleday/Currency.

Sergiovanni, Thomas J. 1992. *Moral leadership: Getting to the heart of school improvement.* San Francisco: Jossey-Bass.

————. 1996. *Leadership for the schoolhouse: How is it different? Why is it important?* San Francisco: Jossey-Bass.

————. 2000. *The lifeworld of leadership: Creating culture, community, and personal meaning in our schools.* San Francisco: Jossey-Bass.

————. 2005. *Strengthening the heartbeat: Leading and learning together in schools.* San Francisco: Jossey-Bass.

_____. 2007. *Rethinking leadership: A collection of articles.* 2nd ed. Thousand Oaks, CA: Corwin Press.

Servage, Laura. 2008. Critical and transformative practices in professional learning communities. *Teacher Education Quarterly* 35, no. 1:63–77.

Shank, Melody J. 2005. Common space, common time, common work. *Educational Leadership* 62, no. 8 (May): 16–19.

Strauss, Robert P., and Elizabeth A. Sawyer. 1986. Some new evidence on teacher and student competencies. *Economics of Education Review* 5, no. 1:41–48.

Strong, James. n.d. *Strong's exhaustive concordance of the Bible.* Peabody, MA: Hendrickson.

Stronks, Gloria Goris, and Doug Blomberg, eds. 1993. *A vision with a task: Christian schooling for responsive discipleship.* Grand Rapids, MI: Baker Books.

Tappert, Theodore G., ed. 1967. *Selected writings of Martin Luther: 1529–1546.* Minneapolis, MN: Fortress Press.

Van Brummelen, Harro. 2009. *Walking with God in the classroom: Christian approaches to teaching and learning.* 3rd ed. Colorado Springs, CO: Purposeful Design Publications.

Vander Ark, Daniel R. 2000. *From mission to measurement.* Grand Rapids, MI: Christian Schools International.

Van Dyk, John. 2001. Bridging the gaps: Exploring the relations between theory, educational philosophy, teacher reflection, and classroom practice. Discussion paper, Dordt College, Sioux Center, IA.

Wei, Ruth Chung, Linda Darling-Hammond, Alethea Andree, Nikole Richardson, Stelios Orphanos, 2009. *Professional learning in the learning profession: A status report on teacher development in the U.S. and abroad.* Dallas, TX: National Staff Development Council.

Weld, Thomas, and Hugh Peter, eds. 1643. *New England's first fruits.* London. Quoted in Cubberley 1920, 292.

Wells, Caryn, and William G. Keane. 2008. Building capacity for professional learning communities through a systems approach: A toolbox for superintendents. *AASA Journal of Scholarship and Practice* 4, no. 4 (Winter): 24–32.

Western, Simon. 2008. *Leadership: A critical text*. London: Sage.

Westminster Christian Academy. 1997. Philosophy of curriculum. Working paper, Westminster Christian Academy, St. Louis, MO.

Williams, Jackie S. 2003. Why great teachers stay. *Educational Leadership* 60, no. 8 (May): 71–74.

Wilson, Susan M., Robert E. Floden, and Joan Ferrini-Mundy. 2001. *Teacher preparation research: Current knowledge, gaps, and recommendations*. Seattle, WA: Center for the Study of Teaching and Policy. http://depts.washington.edu/ctpmail/PDFs/TeacherPrep-WFFM-02-2001.pdf.

Wong, Harry K. 2002a. Induction: The best form of professional development. *Educational Leadership* 59, no. 6 (March): 52–54.

———. 2002b. Play for keeps. *Principal Leadership*, September, 55–58.

———. 2003. Save millions—Train and support new teachers: Schools spend $50,000 to replace each new teacher who quits. *School Business Affairs*, November, 19–22. http://www.newteacher.com/pdf/SBAffair_Nov03_wong.pdf.

———. 2004. Induction programs that keep new teachers teaching and improving. *NASSP Bulletin* 88, no. 638 (March): 45.

Zachary, Lois J. 2000. *The mentor's guide: Facilitating effective learning relationships*. San Francisco: Jossey-Bass.